CW00546335

THE
MARRIAGE
COURSE

Leaders' Guide

First published 2000
Reprinted 2001
Revised 2004

Published by Alpha International, Holy Trinity Brompton, Brompton Road, London, SW7 1JA

Contents

A: What is involved?
The aim of the course   1
Who is the course for?   2
The design of the course   3
The set-up of the room   4
The structure of an evening   5

B: Setting up a course
Who should lead it?   9
Professional help   10
Establishing a task force   10
Resources required   11
Preparing to lead an evening   11
Feedback   12
How to promote the course   13
Registering a course   14

C: An overview and timetable for each evening
Session 1 – Building Strong Foundations   15
Session 2 – The Art of Communication   19
Session 3 – Resolving Conflict   23
Session 4 – The Power of Forgiveness   25
Session 5 – Parents and In-Laws   27
Session 6 – Good Sex   31
Session 7 – Love in Action   35
Session 8 – The Marriage Course Party   39

Appendices
Appendix 1 – Suggested room set-up   41
Appendix 2 – Examples of suitable music   42
Appendix 3 – The Marriage Course Invitation   45
Appendix 4 – The Marriage Course Questionnaire   46
Appendix 5 – Recommended books   48

A: WHAT IS INVOLVED?

1) The aim of the course

With two out of every five marriages breaking down in the UK, thirty–five per cent of them within the first six years, the institution of marriage is under threat today. Some are suggesting that the traditional goal of life-long marriage should be abandoned in favour of an arrangement that makes 'coupling' and 'un-coupling' as easy as possible.

Yet marriage remains of vital importance as the foundation of a stable society. Marriage is the ideal God-given basis of family life, particularly because children learn best what committed, loving relationships are all about through their experience of the commitment between their mother and father.

Many people get married without ever having seen a model of how to build a marriage. They lack the tools that enable them to remain connected. If they stay together, they may exist side by side under the same roof but lose the intimacy between them. They have been embarrassed to seek help or have not known where to find it.

Christianity has much to offer. The Bible not only defines what marriage is but also teaches us how to build a marriage over a lifetime. Biblical principles for strong relationships are desperately needed and increasingly sought after in our society.

The aim of The Marriage Course is to enable married couples to build a healthy marriage that will last a lifetime. Over eight evenings spent together they find out new things about each other, and new things about themselves. They have the opportunity to talk about issues that have been swept under the carpet in the rush of daily life. They discover what makes their partner feel loved. They have the time to discuss ways they have caused each other pain and discover how to heal hurt. They recognise the sources of pressure on their relationship.

Some learn new skills for communicating and resolving conflict. Others make changes in their lifestyle in order to nurture their marriage. And they grow closer to each other in the process.

A couple's privacy is always respected. There is no requirement to disclose anything personal to a third party. But they are expected to talk to each other.

We have been developing The Marriage Course at Holy Trinity Brompton since September 1996. We run the course three times a year and well over a thousand couples have now done it. Our experience has shown us again and again that any marriage can be strengthened through doing the course when both husband and wife are prepared to work at their relationship together.

The Marriage Course is designed for others to use whether in a big group or with one or two other couples in their own home. Our hope and prayer is that many courses will be established so that any couple anywhere can find the help and encouragement they need to build their marriage.

2) Who is the course for?

The Marriage Course is for any couple who want to work together at their relationship. Some couples who have attended the course have been married for less than two years, while others for more than thirty.

The course is beneficial and enjoyable for those whose marriage is already strong. It also helps couples who are going through difficulties. They are able to re-open communication in a guided and constructive way. Some couples who are separated or divorced have used the course as a way of trying to get back together.

While the course emphasises and explains the unique nature of marriage, we welcome 'co-habiting' couples if they have been together for some time. Those who have been together for less than two years and are thinking of marriage are encouraged to come on our Marriage Preparation Course.

Although the course is based on Christian principles and led by Christians, it is very suitable for those with no Christian faith or church background. We use our own experience in Session 3 to speak of the difference that having God at the centre makes to a marriage.

Those without a Christian faith are often interested and attracted by what they hear. They are not required to do or say anything that would conflict with their own beliefs. For some such couples it has provided the first contact with the church and we have invited them to follow up The Marriage Course by doing an Alpha course together.[1]

3) The design of the course:

The length: The course takes place over eight evenings (including The Marriage Course Party – see below). It works best when at least the first four sessions take place on consecutive weeks. The remaining four sessions may be held a fortnight apart to allow more time for the couples to put the principles of the course into practice on their own. The course is long enough to allow for real change in a relationship. Bad habits can be broken and good habits formed.

'Homework': During the periods between sessions, couples are able to put what they have learnt into practice. Each session includes some 'homework'. This consists of exercises that the guests are encouraged to do at home to help them to continue their communication in a constructive way.

The Marriage Course Party (Session 8): The eighth evening of the course (ideally two weeks after the seventh session) is a supper party to which couples on the course can invite other married couples along to a relaxed evening. The couples sit together over an extended dinner. Before coffee and tea are served, there is a talk on what makes a marriage work and a brief description of The Marriage Course. Three or four couples who are on the current course are interviewed and asked to share some of the ways in which their marriage has benefited from doing The Marriage Course. An invitation to the next course is given to all the guests.

---

[1] The Alpha Course is a 15-session practical introduction to the Christian faith designed primarily for non-churchgoers and new Christians. It is run in over 8,000 churches in the UK and over 28,000 churches worldwide.

The party has been used effectively as an opportunity for anybody in the church, whether married or single, to invite married couples to an enjoyable evening and to hear about the course. It could be put on a few weeks before the start of the first course as a way of attracting guests.

The cost: The cost of the course covers the meal and the materials. We ask the guests to pay when they register for the course. (Bursaries are available and some couples make a contribution to the bursary fund when they register.)

This avoids having to collect money each evening and encourages a greater commitment to do the whole course. If the cost is thought to be prohibitive or off-putting, a donation for the meal could be collected when the guests arrive for each session.

Absentees: If a couple is unable to make an evening, we give them an audio tape of the talk. (These should be purchased in advance by the course leader.) The money they have paid for the meal covers the cost of the tape.

4) The set-up of the room (see Appendix 1)

The environment is crucial to the success of the course. The attention to detail is greatly appreciated by the guests and causes them to feel that their marriage is of high value. The setting up is done before the guests arrive. The atmosphere needs to be warm and welcoming so that the guests feel relaxed and safe.

There is a table for registration near the door with a list of the guests, Marriage Course Manuals and name labels (if the course is large enough to warrant these).

The room is arranged with small tables (enough for one per couple) with tablecloths, table napkins and candles. There is sufficient space between the tables for each couple to be able to speak freely without being overheard by others. If the course is being run in a home, couples may use different rooms during the long discussion time to allow sufficient privacy.

If there is sufficient space, chairs are arranged in pairs at the front of the room where the guests sit for the initial talks and short breaks. Otherwise they sit at the tables for the whole session.

There is low lighting (except during the talks) and music is played during the meal and when the couples are doing the written exercises and talking together at the tables.

The music system and choice of music needs to allow an even volume and distribution of sound in order to enable each husband and wife to hear one another, but not be overheard by another couple. (See Appendix 2 for examples of suitable music.)

There is a display of recommended books on marriage. The simplest system is to have demonstration copies only and order forms from the church bookstall or local Christian bookshop. These can be sent or collected at the following session. (See Appendix 5 for our list of recommended books.)

5) The structure of an evening (for Sessions 1-7)

The whole evening, including the meal, lasts up to two hours and forty minutes but can be shortened by reducing the length of the talks.

Welcome: Guests are welcomed warmly as they arrive by at least one of the leaders, and are given a Marriage Course Manual. If the course has more than four or five couples, name badges are helpful. A cold non-alcoholic drink is served and the guests are introduced to each other. Many of them are apprehensive on the first evening and the welcome is part of the reassurance they need.

The meal (35 minutes): This contributes to the effect of the whole evening. Guests have the choice either to sit alone as a couple or to meet other couples around small candle-lit tables over an enjoyable meal. Some tables are laid for two people, others for four or six. (For a smaller course in a home the couples may eat together round a table or buffet style depending on the size and layout of the home.) They have a main course only as coffee, tea and dessert are served later in the evening.

Many people who have done the course have commented that the meal has made it feel like a special 'evening out' as a couple. If, however, arranging the meal proves impossible, the course may be run without it as long as the guests are given something to drink as they arrive and something to eat later in the evening (during the long discussion).

Notices and review (up to 10 minutes): We start with notices and then a review of the previous session or sessions. On Session 1 each couple is given the option of telling another couple where they met and what first attracted them to each other, including aspects other than the purely physical! This is the only time we ask them to divulge anything personal to another couple. We stress that it is optional, intended to be fun and that they are not to embarrass their partner.

From Session 2, husbands and wives tell their partner what they remember from the previous session(s) that was of particular importance to them.

On Session 7 each person is asked to fill in the questionnaire to review the course.

Talk (30 to 60 minutes): The talk starts with some humour and is broken up at intervals with opportunities for husband and wife to talk to one another, sometimes with the aid of an exercise. (These breaks during the talks last between 5 and 10 minutes and the guests remain where they are.)

The talks can be done with the videos which give clear instructions of the timing and length of the pauses when the couples discuss an issue.

Testimony (5 minutes): A couple who have done a previous course talk about the difference this particular session has made in their own marriage. On the first course, a testimony could be used from The Marriage Course Street Interviews and Testimonies Video.

Long discussion (at the tables) (30 to 40 minutes): Each couple needs a table to themselves at this stage of the evening. There is background music. If the course is being run in a home, couples may need to go to separate rooms to allow sufficient privacy. They do the exercises that have been set, each writing down their thoughts and then discussing together what they have written.

Coffee, tea, homemade biscuits, muffins, brownies or fruit are served by the leaders and other helpers as soon as possible to allow the guests to spend the majority of their time together uninterrupted.

As the exercises often raise issues that are very personal and may be upsetting, privacy is important.

Concluding remarks and prayer (10 to 40 minutes): The guests are asked to stay where they are for the final section (unless of course they are in different rooms).

At the end of the evening the guests are encouraged to arrange 'marriage time' for the coming week. From Session 3 they are given the opportunity either to pray for their husband or wife or to express their support for each other in some other way.

The leaders finish the evening with a short closing prayer. Some couples might want to stay to continue discussing issues with each other or with the leaders. It is important that other couples feel free to leave straight away.

B: SETTING UP A COURSE

1) Who should lead it?

The Marriage Course should be led by a Christian couple who have the desire to see marriages strengthened and who feel compassion for those who are struggling. They should have the support of their church leader. If they are giving the talks themselves they will need to have some experience of leading groups and a willingness to share openly from their own marriage.

It is important that the leaders have first been through all the material themselves, doing the exercises as a couple, discussing the issues raised and seeking to apply the principles of the course to their own marriage. We recommend they do the course with the videos with one or two other couples whom they know well. There should be a commitment to continue to build their own marriage and a willingness to be accountable to another couple. There should be no major unresolved issues between them when they start to lead a course.

Leading the course will often strengthen the leaders' own marriage through reminding them of important principles and through their working together, but it is not uncommon for their relationship to come under pressure during the course. It is therefore important that they have others who are praying for them and to whom they can turn for encouragement and support.

For larger courses (with more than about ten couples) the leaders will need at least one other mature Christian couple to support them in providing specific help for guests who request it. These 'support couples' should also have done The Marriage Course and may give a testimony on the current course. This will help the guests to get to know them. Their aim in talking to individual couples is to help them to apply the principles of the course to their own situation.

2) Professional help

The leaders should know when and where to refer couples for professional help if the issues that arise are beyond their own experience and training or the capabilities of their team. This might be the case where a guest needs counselling as a result of childhood abuse or where there are complex sexual issues. (The bibliography in The Marriage Book gives some suggestions of organisations that may help to find local counsellors.) Details of their availability and the cost (if any) can be left on the book table for any guests who want to find professional help more anonymously.

3) Establishing a 'taskforce'

The taskforce supports all aspects of the course including:

- setting up the room
- preparing the meal
- welcoming guests as they arrive
- serving the meal
- clearing and washing up
- resetting the tables after the meal
- re-lighting the candles when needed
- helping to serve coffee and tea
- turning the music on and off

The number of helpers required on the taskforce will depend on the size of the course. Even with a course of two or three couples the leaders will benefit from having others who can help them so that they are free to give their full attention to the guests.

On the second and subsequent courses, guests from previous courses are invited to help on one or more evenings. Many couples are glad of the opportunity to give something back as well as to hear a particular talk again.

For The Marriage Course Party a larger taskforce is required to serve the meal (two courses), clear away and hand round tea and coffee.

4) Resources required

- The Marriage Course Leaders' Guide
- A Marriage Course Manual for each of the guests (two per couple)
- The Marriage Course Video Set (for talks, testimonies and diagrams)
- The Marriage Course Street Interviews and Testimonies Video
  (for those giving live talks who would like to use pre-recorded testimonies)
- The Marriage Course Speakers' Notes and Presentation Slides CD-ROM
  (if giving live talks)
- Individual audio tapes of each session for couples who miss an evening
- The Marriage Book by Nicky and Sila Lee (Alpha International, 2000)
- Music (suitable music is suggested in Appendix 2)
- Tables and chairs
- Tablecloths, candles, candleholders and table napkins
- Food, coffee and tea-making facilities
- A PowerPoint or overhead projector (not essential, but helpful for displaying diagrams from the CD-ROM)
- Lectern or other stand for speakers' notes
  (for larger courses only when the speakers need to stand to give the talks)

5) Preparing to lead an evening

The course can be run using the video set. The videos will need to be paused when husbands and wives are discussing an issue. The instructions for the pauses are clearly marked. These breaks last between 5 and 40 minutes. It is worth checking how long the video recorder can be on pause before it automatically turns itself off.

If you are giving the talks yourselves, start your preparation at least a week before. (Speakers' notes of the talks are available on CD-ROM. These may be adapted as you include illustrations from your own marriage, and may be shortened.)

We have found it helpful to prepare the evening together.

- Start your preparation with a prayer
- Watch the video or listen to the audio tape of the particular session and read the relevant section of The Marriage Book
- Talk through the plan for the session and any concerns you may have
- Decide who will do each section of the talks
- Work out what you are going to share from your own experience
- Adjust the speakers' notes (if using the CD-ROM) adding illustrations from your own marriage
- Go through this with each other to make sure that you are agreed about what you will include. Do not include anything that would offend, belittle or otherwise upset your partner
- Make sure that you feel comfortable with the material and are familiar with the exercises

If another couple who have already done The Marriage Course are giving a testimony, it is worth speaking to them beforehand to make sure they are prepared. The main aim of the testimony is to illustrate the benefits of the session from the couple's own experience. It should last about five minutes. Interviewing them enables the leader to guide what they say and to limit the length if necessary. Both husband and wife should speak. Find out beforehand what difference the session made to their marriage and ask questions that will keep the testimony personal and helpful to the guests. (Natural humour is a great asset.) Some helpful questions are:

- Why did you come on The Marriage Course?
  Or: How would you describe your marriage when you started the course?
- What happened on this session?
- What difference has it made to your relationship since then?

6) Feedback

A questionnaire has been developed to be distributed on the seventh evening (see Appendix 4). This serves as a review of the course for the guests and provides helpful feedback for the leaders to know how to make the course more effective the next time.

7) How to promote the course

We need to remove the stigma involved in doing a marriage course. It is not an admission of failure nor an indication that a couple's marriage is in trouble. In the same way that many people today do courses to enhance their skills in management, computing or mechanics, this is a course to enhance their marriage.

You may run the course within your church or within the local community. Whatever the setting, the message is the same: 'The Marriage Course is for anyone who is married to help them to get the most out of their marriage. It is based on Christian principles but is very suitable for non-churchgoers. It gives couples skills to grow together and to deepen their intimacy with each other. And it is fun!'

Make clear that couples will not be required to divulge anything about their own marriage to anybody else, but they will be encouraged to talk to each other.

There is a great advantage in running two or three courses a year as most guests come on the recommendation of others who have already done it.

After the first course, a testimony at a Sunday service by a couple who have done the course, enjoyed it and benefited from it, will encourage others to come. It is important that the testimonies are kept personal by asking such questions as:

- Why did you decide to do The Marriage Course?
- What happened on the course?
- What difference has it made to your marriage?

Create a plan for publicising your course. Allow at least eight weeks before the course begins. Print invitations (see the example in Appendix 3) and encourage people to give these to their friends. Ask if an announcement may be made in your church and possibly in other churches nearby. Use publicity through a local paper, schools or doctors' surgeries if you are ready to reach a wider audience.

The Marriage Course Party may be held a few weeks before starting the first course. Invitations to the party can be given to any married couple and married or single people are encouraged to invite their married friends.

8) Registering a course

If you are planning to run The Marriage Course please let us know at The Marriage Course, Holy Trinity Brompton, Brompton Road, London SW7 1JA or via our website themarriagecourse.org. This will enable us to support you in the future and direct any enquiring couples who live in your area to your course.

C: AN OVERVIEW AND TIMETABLE FOR EACH EVENING

Session 1 – Building Strong Foundations

1) Overview:

Closeness in marriage must be nurtured. It is essential we find time together and understand each other's needs. This session causes couples to look at their lifestyle and its effect upon their marriage, and to learn more about each other's needs and desires.

2) Resources:

The Marriage Book – Section 1

The Marriage Course – Video tape 1, Session 1

The Marriage Course – Audio tape 1

The Marriage Course Speakers' Notes and Presentation Slides CD-ROM – Session 1

3) Checklist:

A manual for each guest

Video projector, screen and video of session (for talk and / or 'vox pops' and testimony)

Music – during the meal
        – during the discussions
        – at the end

Name labels

Suitable lighting

Cold drink

Food

Tea, coffee and dessert

Tables, tablecloths and chairs

Table napkins, candles and candleholders

Spare pens

Book table

Speakers' stand

Guest attendance list

Visual aids (for live talk, Session 1 only):
        – sheets of coloured paper (separate and stuck together)
        – jug of water, glass and tray

PowerPoint or overhead projector ('OHP') – for live talks only (optional)

PowerPoint or OHP slides from CD-ROM – for live talks only (optional)

4) Timetable:

Times:

From 6.30pm   Be ready! (Guests often arrive early on the first evening)
Welcome and offer a cold drink

7.00   The Meal

7.35   Notices

- 'Please write your name on your manual'

- 'If you get stuck at any point on the course please tell us.
We or another couple would be delighted to see you privately'

- 'Let us know if you can't come for one of the evenings and we will
give/send you the tape'

- 'Relax! You will not be required to disclose anything private about
your relationship after the next exercise'

- 'For a bit of fun, and only if you would like to, tell one other couple where
you met and what first attracted you to each other (including aspects other
than the purely physical!)'

7.45   Talk – *What is marriage?*

8.10   Testimony – (live or from the video for Session 1 or
The Marriage Course Street Interviews and Testimonies Video)

8.15   Exercise – *Taking stock of your marriage* (at the tables)

8.45   Give a five minute warning before starting the next section
of the talk

8.50   Talk – *Making time for each other*

9.05   Husbands and wives tell each other the best times they
have had together as a couple, including when, where
and what they were doing

9.10   Talk – *Nurturing one another*

9.20   Exercise – *Knowing me, knowing you*

9.30   Conclusion

• Explain and encourage the 'homework'

• Give about 3 minutes for couples to organise 'marriage time' for the coming week

9.35   End with a short prayer eg

'Lord, thank you that you are the God of love. Please help us to love each other more and more. May we grow in our understanding of each other's needs and show love through seeking to meet those needs each day this week. Amen'

Session 2 – The Art of Communication

1) Overview:

Listening is a skill that can and must be learned for a strong marriage. Couples practise communicating their feelings and listening effectively to each other.

2) Resources:

The Marriage Book – Section 2

The Marriage Course – Video tape 1, Session 2

The Marriage Course – Audio tape 2

The Marriage Course Speakers' Notes and Presentation Slides CD-ROM – Session 2

3) Checklist:

As for Session 1

Spare Marriage Course Manuals
(for guests to borrow if they have forgotten theirs)

An issue that one of you has thought of to use for the leaders' demonstration of *Effective listening*

Two chairs for the leaders' demonstration

A handkerchief or table napkin for the leaders' demonstration

4) Timetable:

From 6.45pm   Welcome guests with a drink

7.00   The Meal

7.35   Notices

• 'Please bring your manuals for each session – there are spare ones for any who have forgotten theirs'

• 'If you get stuck on the course at any point please let us know'

• Review

• Remind of the importance of 'marriage time'

• Remind of the importance of understanding each other's desires: 'We can't assume our desires are the same. I can't assume I know my partner's desires. I can't assume they instinctively know mine'

• 'Without looking in your manual, tell your husband or wife their top 3 desires from the exercise in Session 1 *Knowing me, knowing you* to see if you have remembered correctly'

• 'Find out from your husband or wife what was most important for them from Session 1'

7.45   Talk – *Introduction – Effective communication –The importance of talking - The importance of listening*

8.00   Exercise – *The power of listening*

[8.04   Feedback – Collect short answers to the first two questions in the exercise from the group as a whole (for live talks only)]

8.05   Talk – *Hindrances to listening*

8.25   Exercise – *A significant memory*

8.30   Talk – *Principles for effective listening*

8.35   Leaders' demonstration of effective listening

• Before the evening, one of you needs to have thought of an issue that you have not previously discussed. (Do not choose an issue that would be deeply hurtful or embarrassing for your husband or wife)

• This person holds the handkerchief or table napkin to remind both of you whose issue it is

• Using the five principles for effective listening, demonstrate in front of the whole group what effective listening looks like and sounds like (as on the video and audio tapes)

8.45	Testimony (live or from the video for Session 2)
8.50	Exercise – *Effective listening (at the tables)*
9.25	Conclusion
9.35	Give 3 minutes to organise marriage time for the coming week
9.38	End with a short prayer eg

'Lord, thank you that you are always listening to us. Help us to be good at listening to each other that we may grow in our understanding and support of one another. Amen'

Session 3 – Resolving Conflict

1) Overview:

Problems can strengthen a marriage when a couple tackles them together. Their togetherness is helped by expressing their appreciation of each other, recognising their differences of temperament, learning to negotiate disagreements and praying for each other.

2) Resources:

The Marriage Book – Section 4

The Marriage Course – Video tape 2, Session 3

The Marriage Course – Audio tape 3

The Marriage Course Speakers' Notes and Presentation Slides CD-ROM – Session 3

3) Checklist:

As for Session 1

Spare guest manuals

4) Timetable:

From 6.45pm   Welcome guests with a drink

7.00   The Meal

7.35   Review

- 'Tell your husband or wife one occasion over this last week when they met one of your requests from Session 1, Exercise 2 – *Knowing me, knowing you*'

- 'Tell your husband or wife what you learnt about yourself last week'

7.40   Talk – *Introduction – Expressing our appreciation of each other*

8.00   Exercise 1 – *Showing appreciation*

8.10   Talk – *Recognising our differences*

8.20   Exercise 2 – *Recognise your differences*

8.30   Talk – *Negotiating areas of conflict*

8.40   Testimony (live or from the video for Session 3)

8.50   Exercise 3 – *Changing our behaviour* (at the tables)

9.15   Give a five minute warning before starting the next section of the talk

9.20   Conclusion – Learning to pray together

9.35   Give couples the option:

- either to ask their husband or wife to tell them one thing they can pray for and then to pray for each other aloud or silently

- or to ask each other for another way in which they could show support over something the other is worried about

9.40   Close with a short prayer

Session 4 – The Power of Forgiveness

1) Overview:

Apology and forgiveness are essential to restore trust and intimacy when we have hurt each other. This session helps couples to put this into practice for past and present hurts.

2) Resources:

The Marriage Book – Section 5

The Marriage Course – Video tape 2, Session 4

The Marriage Course – Audio tape 4

The Marriage Course Speakers' Notes and Presentation Slides CD-ROM – Session 4

3) Checklist:

As for Session 1

Spare guest manuals

Visual aid (for live talk): spiral notebook

4) Timetable:

From 6.45pm   Welcome guests with a drink

7.00   The Meal

7.35   Review

• Review of Sessions 1-3 – ask couples to tell their husband or wife which point from the reminder section in the manual they consider the most important for their marriage

• 'Discuss whether over the past two weeks you have managed to work through problems together rather than attacking and criticising each other'

7.40   Talk – *How can intimacy be lost?* – *How can intimacy be restored?*

                   1)   Identify hurt
                   2)   Apologise

8.10   Testimony (live or from the video for Session 4)

8.15   Explain exercise – and pray a short prayer asking for God's help

8.20   Exercise – *Identifying unresolved hurt* (at the tables)

8.55   Give a five minute warning before doing the conclusion

9.00   Conclusion – *How can intimacy be restored? (cont.)*

                   3)   Forgiveness
                   4)   Start again together

9.25   Encourage couples to do the homework as this completes the process begun in the exercise *Identifying unresolved hurt.*
Give an opportunity for couples to pray for their husband or wife or to express their support for each other in some other way

9.30   Close the session with a short prayer and then encourage couples to organise marriage time for the coming week

Session 5 – Parents and In-laws

1) Overview:

Couples are helped to recognise how their family background affects the way they relate to each other. They also consider how to build a good and healthy relationship with their parents, in-laws and wider family now.

Leaders need to be aware that this session can bring up unresolved hurt from the past which may take longer to resolve than the course allows.

2) Resources:

The Marriage Book – Section 6

The Marriage Course – Video tape 3, Session 5

The Marriage Course – Audio tape 5

The Marriage Course Speakers' Notes and Presentation Slides CD-ROM – Session 5

3) Checklist:

As for Session 1

Spare Marriage Course Guest Manuals

Bag of 10 small coins on each table (for the exercise **Reflect on your upbringing**)

4) Timetable:

From 6.45pm   Welcome guests with a drink

7.00   The Meal

7.35   Notices

  • Encourage couples to ask for help if they get stuck over an issue that the course has raised, particularly as a result of this evening

Review

  • 'Looking at this week's reminder section in the manual, tell your partner either, *"You're good at....,"* or, *"I need to ......,"* but not, *"You need to..."'*

7.40   Talk – *Introduction – Growing up – Creating healthy family relationships points 1 –5*

8.15   Husbands and wives discuss the first five principles for creating healthy family relationships

8.20   Talk – *Creating healthy family relationships point 6*

8.30   Testimony (live or from the video for Session 5)

8.35   Explain exercise – *Reflect on your upbringing* (demonstrating how to use the coins with the OHP, if available)

8.40   Exercise – *Reflect on your upbringing* (at the tables)

9.10   Conclusion – *Healing childhood pain*

9.20   To help those who still carry pain from their childhood, lead the guests in a prayer expressing forgiveness towards parents or others (as in *The Marriage Book* Chapter 15).
Then ask God to heal the hurt

9.25   Give the guests the opportunity to pray for their husband or wife or to express support in some other way.
(Offer to talk and / or pray with any of the guests who would

like to at the end of the session. They might want to arrange to do this at another time during the week)

9.30   Close the session with a short prayer and then encourage couples to organise marriage time for the coming week

Session 6 – Good Sex

1) Overview:

Sexual intimacy needs to be worked at and developed. Couples are able to communicate about their expectations and disappointments and to recognise where they need to make changes.

Leaders who give their own talks need to be able to talk about this subject without embarrassment and with some gentle humour. This helps the guests to address this area of their marriage with openness.

2) Resources:

The Marriage Book – Section 7

The Marriage Course – Video tape 3, Session 6

The Marriage Course – Audio tape 6

The Marriage Course Speakers' Notes and Presentation Slides CD-ROM – Session 6

3) Checklist:

As for Session 1

Spare guest manuals

The Marriage Course Party invitations

4) Timetable:

From 6.45pm   Welcome guests with a drink

7.00   The Meal (put a Marriage Course Party Invitation on each chair and make more invitations available)

7.35   Notices

• Encourage guests to invite another married couple to the supper party at the end of the course. Explain what will happen on the evening. Encourage them to take more invitations if they want to invite more than one couple

Review

• Talk as a couple about: 'What was most important for you from the last session on parents and in-laws?'

7.40   Talk – *Introduction and Six qualities of great lovers*
1) The importance of communication

8.05   Husband and wife ask each other what has been important for them so far in this session

8.10   Talk – *Six qualities of great lovers (continued)*
2) The importance of tenderness
3) The importance of responsiveness
4) The importance of romance

8.25   Husband and wife tell each other the most romantic times they have had together

8.30   Talk – *Six qualities of great lovers (continued)*
5) The importance of anticipation
6) The importance of variety

8.40   Testimony (live or from the video for Session 6)

8.50   Exercise – *Talking about sex* (at the tables)

9.20   Conclusion – *Protecting our marriage*

9.30   Give the guests an opportunity to pray for their partner or to express support in some other way. (Suggest that this might be an appropriate moment to apologise and / or express forgiveness to each other if they have hurt each other through their sexual relationship)

9.35   Close with a short prayer and then encourage couples to organise marriage time for the coming week.

Session 7 – Love in Action

1) Overview:

There are five ways of expressing love – through words, time, touch, presents and actions. Couples discover which expression of love is most important for their partner and how to show love to them consistently in this way.

2) Resources:

The Marriage Book – Section 3

The Marriage Course – Video tape 4, Session 7

The Marriage Course – Audio tape 7

The Marriage Course Speakers' Notes and Presentation Slides CD-ROM – Session 7

The Five Love Languages by Gary Chapman (Northfield 1995)

3) Checklist:

Spare guest manuals

Questionnaire (one per guest)

Extra Marriage Course Party invitations

Invitations to the next Marriage Course

Presents for the 'taskforce'

4) Timetable:

From 6.45pm   Welcome guests with a drink

7.00   The Meal (put a questionnaire on each chair)

7.35   Review

• Ask the guests to fill in the questionnaire.
They will complete the final section at the end of the evening

7.45   Notices

• Thank the taskforce and give small presents to those who have helped each week, especially if they are unmarried

• Remind guests of the opportunity to invite other married couples to
The Marriage Course Party

• Encourage the guests to take invitations to the next *Marriage Course* to give to others (particularly if they are unable to come to the party)

• Encourage the guests to seek further help if the course has revealed areas of ongoing difficulties. (Having details of counsellors, including one who specialises in sex therapy, on the book table can help a guest or couple who may be embarrassed to talk to the leaders)

• Encourage them to finish any homework they have not managed during the course

• Give guests information of how to explore the Christian faith further if they would like to (eg make *Alpha* invitations available on the book table and explain that the *Alpha* course is run along very similar lines to *The Marriage Course* except that the discussions following the talk take place in small groups)

7.50   Talk – *Introduction, Loving words, Thoughtful presents, Physical affection*

8.20   Husbands and wives tell each other what has been most significant for them (or what has been the best present they have received from each other)

8.25	Talk – *Quality time, Kind actions*
8.35	Testimony – (live or from the video for Session 7)
8.40	Explain exercise – *Discover your partner's and your own 'love language(s)'*
8.45	Exercise – *Discover your partner's and your own 'love language(s)'* (at the tables)
9.15	Ask guests to complete the questionnaires
9.20	Conclusion
9.30	Close the session with a short prayer and then encourage couples to organise marriage time
	Collect questionnaires before the guests leave

Session 8 - The Marriage Course Party

1) Overview:

The aim is for the guests to have an enjoyable evening, to hear about *The Marriage Course* and to learn something that will be of benefit to their marriage, whether or not they decide to do the course themselves. The meal is extended, the talk is shorter than for other sessions and there are no exercises.

The party is an effective way of introducing couples to *The Marriage Course* as most people are more likely to come to one evening with a talk about marriage than to join a course. Many of the guests subsequently come on *The Marriage Course*.

2) Resources:

The Marriage Course – Video tape 4, Session 8

The Marriage Course – Audio tape 8 (2nd edition only)

3) Checklist:

Video projector and large screen (if using *The Marriage Course* Street Interviews and Testimonies video)

Music (before and after the talk)

Cold drink

Food

Tea and coffee

Tables (for about 8-10 people each)

Tablecloths, table napkins, candles and candleholders

Flowers

Invitations to the next *Marriage Course*

4) Timetable:

7.30	Welcome guests with a drink
8.00	The Meal
8.50	Talk – *What makes a marriage work?*
9.25	Testimonies by 3 or 4 couples who have been on the current course (or from the video set for Session 8)
9.35	Conclusion

Guests are served coffee or tea and given an invitation to the next Marriage Course

Appendix 1: Suggested room set-up

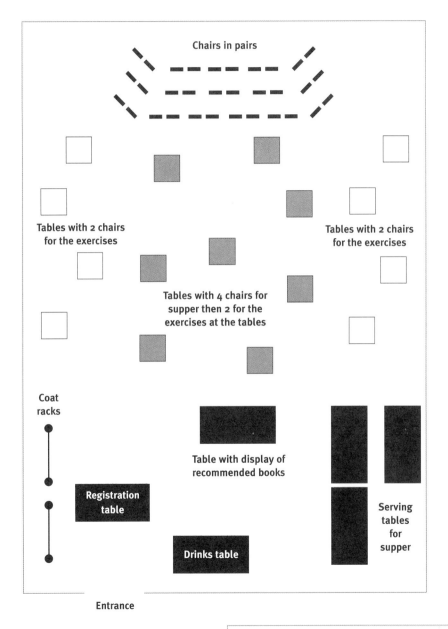

Appendix 2:
Examples of suitable music

The background music played while the couples are doing the exercises and discussing issues needs to be of an even volume. Otherwise, during the quieter sections, the couples will be overheard and, during the louder sections, they won't be able to hear their partner. We use a variety of classical and contemporary music, aiming to match the mood of the music to the nature of the exercise.

At the end of the evening, the music needs to be reasonably quiet as, from Session 3, the guests are given the opportunity to pray for their husband or wife.

The following list is for example only. The type of music used should be adjusted to match the musical taste of the guests.

Session 1

During the meal and short exercises Mozart – Symphonie Concertanti K.364 and K.297b and Rondo – K.269

Long exercise C.P.E. Bach – Flute Concertos

End Andy Piercy & Dave Clifton – 'Psalms, hymns & spiritual songs' (track 3)

Session 2

During the meal and short exercises Enya – 'Shepherd Moons'

Long exercise Albinoni – '12 Concertos, op. 9'

End Albinoni – '12 Concertos, op. 9'

Session 3

During the meal and short exercises Mozart – Horn Concerto

Long exercise The choir of Trinity College Cambridge – 'Vocé'

End The choir of Trinity College Cambridge – 'Vocé'

Session 4

During the meal and short exercises 'For the one I love – 12 instrumental songs of love' – Kingsway Music

Long exercise Maire Brennan – 'Perfect Time'

End Solo Christian artist (e.g. Martyn Joseph – 'Being Here' – quieter tracks)

Session 5

During the meal and short exercises Mozart – 'Flute Concertos No. 1 & 2; Flute/Harp Concerto'

Long exercise J S Bach – 'Double Concertos BWV 1043, 1044, 1055, 1060'

End Iona – 'Open Sky' (quieter tracks)

Session 6

During the meal and short exercises The Covenant – 'My Utmost for his Highest'

Long exercise J S and C P E Bach – 'Oboe Concertos'

End Andy Piercy & Dave Clifton – 'Psalms, hymns & spiritual songs' (track 7)

Session 7

During the meal and short exercises Keith Jarrett – 'The Melody At Night, With You'

Long exercise J S Bach – 'Violin Concertos'

End Andy Piercy & Dave Clifton – 'Psalms, hymns & spiritual songs' (track 14)

Appendix 3: The Marriage Course Invitation

THE MARRIAGE COURSE

How to build a healthy marriage that lasts a lifetime

What is The Marriage Course?

The Marriage Course is very practical, giving any married couple the tools to build a strong and healthy marriage that lasts a lifetime.

Over eight evenings spent together couples talk about important issues that can get swept under the carpet in the rush of daily life.

Topics covered include: recognising each other's needs, learning to communicate effectively, resolving conflict, healing past hurt, knowing how to make each other feel loved, relating to parents and in-laws, good sex, making time for each other and having fun together.

Privacy as a couple is always respected. There is no group discussion and no requirement to disclose anything about your relationship to anyone else.

What's involved?

Each evening begins with a candlelit meal. There is then a talk followed by an oppportunity to discuss the topic together as a couple.

The setting is welcoming, relaxed and unthreatening.

Who is it for?

The Marriage Course is for any married couple who want to build a strong and lasting relationship, especially:

- those who want to enhance their marriage
- those in the first five years of marriage
- those at a challenging stage in their marriage eg the birth of a child, a career change, teenagers at home, the 'empty nest'
- those struggling with issues in their marriage

The course, while based on Christian principles, is very helpful for any couple with or without a Christian faith or church background.

Registration Form

Please fill in this form and send it [with your payment if applicable] to the address overleaf to let us know you are coming

Titles   First Names   Surname[s]

Address

Postcode   Daytime telephone   Email

How did you find out about The Marriage Course?

How long have you been married?

Do you belong to a church?   Yes / No   If so which one?

I enclose payment [where applicable] of

We look forward to seeing you

THE MARRIAGE COURSE

How to build a healthy marriage that lasts a lifetime

Appendix 4: The Marriage Course Questionnaire (A4 size - double sided)

The Marriage Course

This questionnaire is a great help in developing the course and we would be grateful if you would answer as thoroughly as you can. **Your answers will remain anonymous.**

Name *(or anonymous if preferred)*: _____ How long married? _____

1. Did you find out about *The Marriage Course* through:
   - Holy Trinity Brompton ☐
   - Personal recommendation ☐
   - Website ☐
   - *The Marriage Book* ☐
   - Another church ☐
   - Other ☐

2. Do you regularly attend church? No ☐ Yes ☐
   If so, which one? _____

3. What issues did you have in your marriage before you started the course?
   _____
   _____

4. In what ways, if any, has the course helped and improved your marriage?
   _____
   _____

5. What were the most important things you learnt on the course?
   _____
   _____

6. What did you enjoy most about the course?
   _____
   _____

7. What did you find most difficult?
   _____
   _____

8. Did you manage to do the homework? No ☐ Yes ☐
   If so, in what ways was it useful?
   _____
   _____

9. Have you managed to build marriage time into your weekly routine during the course?
   If so, how useful has it been?
   _____
   _____

10. How could we improve the course?
    _____
    _____
    _____
    _____

Date	Title	On a scale of 1 - 5, please circle how helpful each evening has been: 1 - not helpful 5 - extremely helpful	Please EXPLAIN why it was helpful or not helpful:
19 January	Building Strong Foundations	1 2 3 4 5	
26 January	The Art of Communication	1 2 3 4 5	
2 February	Resolving Conflict	1 2 3 4 5	
9 February	The Power of Forgiveness	1 2 3 4 5	
23 February	Parents and In-laws	1 2 3 4 5	
1 March	Good Sex	1 2 3 4 5	
8 March	Love in Action	1 2 3 4 5	

Additional comments: _____

_____

_____

_____

Appendix 5: Recommended Books

Gary Chapman, *The Five Love Languages* (Northfield Publishing 1995)

Gary Chapman, *The Other Side of Love – Handling Anger in a Godly Way* (Moody Press 1999)

Gary Chapman, *Hope for the Separated* (Moody Press 1982)

Nicky Gumbel, *30 Days* (Alpha International, 1999)

Nicky Gumbel, *Alpha – Questions of Life* (Kingsway 1993)

Nicky and Sila Lee, *The Marriage Book* (Alpha International 2000)

Mike Mason, *The Mystery of Marriage* (Triangle 1997)

Rob Parsons, *Loving Against the Odds* (Hodder & Stoughton 1994)

Rob Parsons, *The Sixty Minute Marriage* (Hodder & Stoughton 1997)

Mary Pytches, *Yesterday's Child* (Hodder & Stoughton 1990)

Ed and Gaye Wheat, *Intended for Pleasure* (Scripture Union 1979)

Ed and Gaye Wheat, *Love Life for Every Married Couple* (Marshall Pickering 1984)

Philip Yancey, *What's So Amazing About Grace?* (Zondervan Publishing House 1997)

Daily Light (Tyndale Press 1999)

UNHINGED

A Parody

UNHINGED

A Parody

Ian Martin

BLOOMSBURY PUBLISHING
LONDON • OXFORD • NEW YORK • NEW DELHI • SYDNEY

BLOOMSBURY PUBLISHING
Bloomsbury Publishing Plc
50 Bedford Square, London, WC1B 3DP, UK
29 Earlsfort Terrace, Dublin 2, Ireland

BLOOMSBURY, BLOOMSBURY PUBLISHING and the Diana logo are
trademarks of Bloomsbury Publishing Plc

First published in Great Britain 2024

ISBN: HB: 978-1-5266-8663-3; EBOOK: 978-1-5266-8672-5; EPDF: 978-1-5266-8671-8

2 4 6 8 10 9 7 5 3 1

Typeset by Newgen Knowledge Works (P) Ltd., Chennai, India
Printed and bound in Great Britain by CPI Group (UK) Ltd, Croydon CR0 4YY

CONTENTS

Introduction   1

PART ONE: MAKE YOUR OWN TRUTH

July 2019 – July 2022   8

PART TWO: BE MORE BORIS

1   If It Ain't Fixed, Break It   63

2   Think Big, Move On   76

3   Transgress to Progress   86

4   Be Yourself, Repeat Yourself   97

    Epilogue   108

    Notes   110
    Acknowledgements   115

Introduction

People have said some really horrible things about Alexander Boris de Pfeffel Johnson over the years.

'So many *er*s and *ah*s when he speaks, he sounds like a reversing bin lorry, in Latin…'*

'You could see little flashes of violent irritation during the select committee hearing. How *dare* they question him? Didn't they know who he fucking WAS? In the old days he'd be up in the manor house todgering a milkmaid while these inconsequential serfs would be down in the valley tilling his fields…'*

'Johnson did more damage to public trust in one year than anyone else in Parliament for a century, except for Johnson himself the year before, and again the year before that.'*

But enough. It's time for a reset. Time to reconsider the reputation of a man who not only Got Brexit Done but Got Britain Done. Yeah, the country certainly experienced a proper Bullingdon seeing-to. His iconoclastic style completely reconfigured the constitutional and ethical landscape of British politics. The establishment warned him that morality in high office wasn't broken, and that he shouldn't try to fix it. He proved them wrong by breaking it AND fixing it, then breaking it again, several times, just to make sure.

He may, for the time being, have decided on a life largely outside politics. But Boris Johnson's residual DNA remains everywhere in the media and public life. Often detectable only under one of those ultraviolet crime-scene black lights, but it's there all right. He has been a towering figure for decades in the worlds of politics and journalism. Somehow he always gets up again, like the protagonist in that song by Chumbawamba he apparently likes so much.

How might we mere mortals elevate our sad, piffling lives to his level of Olympian greatness? This book will show how Boris's example might guide our own conduct. How to lighten the mood with wholesome self-deprecation, for example. How, when pushed to explain yourself, it's often better just to make something up. Because what, after all, is a lie? What, after all, is the truth? Could you, in a way, simply exchange one for the other? This book will focus on the teachable aspects of his past. It will concentrate on the really good stuff and simply ignore the rest, as one might ignore a discarded girlfriend.

Rethinking the thinkable is the key to unlocking your inner Johnson. All rules, ultimately, are just 'rules'. Better to be a romantic Cavalier than a miserabilist Roundhead. Take a leaf out of Johnson's book: all love in the end is self-love. And the most important forgiveness is self-exoneration. The only narrative that matters is the one you construct yourself, as we'll see in the corrected account of the Downing Street Years.

This book is published as a companion, so-called 'parody' volume to Johnson's own extremely honest account of his time at Number 10. You'll find inspiration here drawn from his illustrious careers: easy-to-recreate social gambits, life rules, and some great excuses that'll get you out of all sorts of tricky situations. It would be easy to dismiss this book as mere parody, but that would be a shame. It might be easier to accept it.

Let's pay Boris the respect he deserves. Let the door to his secrets of life be UNHINGED.

* *Yes, technically this is stuff I've just written inside some quote marks, but it looks better if you think they come from entirely different corroborating sources. What I've done here is create three new truths by making them all up, while keeping the fiction faithful to an inferred half-truthfulness. It's what we can all do. Cheat a little, make life a bit more bearable by being a bit more blurrable. In the end, it doesn't matter. Just do whatever you want. Be More Boris.*

Part One

MAKE YOUR OWN TRUTH

As we have seen, sometimes in examples from Boris Johnson himself, reality is forever chasing the bright elusive butterfly of truth. But is it *so* bad when the truth blurs into a truth-adjacent version?

If we follow the teachings of Sensei Boris we may, er, er, learn the secret WAY of unlocking a very special truth. '*Quid est veritas?*' asked Pontius Pilate, er, did he not, at a pretty TENSE time for all concerned. What is Truth? It's a question that bears repeating and drilling DOWN into, and thoroughly FRACKING. Other people – whether they be the man or, or, or WOMAN on the Clapham omnibus or whether they be hostile inter-rogators at a Parliamentary inquiry – are always keen as mustard, aren't they, to, er, er, discover THE truth, even if that truth is not a truth universally acknowledged. Other people, yes, of course, are, er, er, free to RELATE their versions of events. But the ability to understand what you know to be a plausible counter-version, that's *your* truth. And it's the best truth. The only truth that MATTERS.

We've all read the hurtful, partisan accounts of his diffi-cult – and sometimes heroic – time as prime minister. Yes, that's the 'truth' of his enemies, his mewling rivals. Until now, understanding Prime Minister Boris Johnson has been impossible: we have been faced with a locked door. Behind the locked door: the truth. Guarding that door: the self-appointed media Stasi.

It's time for action! Biff! Clonk! The media guards are out for the count! We must rummage around to find the key. Wait... No key. We'll just have to, er, blow the bloody door off! Luckily, we've brought explosives with us. Hurrah! We set the fuse and stand back. BLAM! We've literally UNHINGED the door to the Classified Truth Room, where the real story will unfold.

In the following pages you will see the Discredited Narrative of the mainstream media. These are the 'facts' as recorded by history. In parallel, at last, the Unhinged Truth of Boris Johnson charts his incredible time in the top job, drawing on actual diary entries absolutely written truthfully at the time, and the laser-etched memories of the man himself.

It's time to fight truth with truth. Behold the Truthmaster at work, and learn. Here then is the media version of reality and the actual, genuine truth.* The FULLY UNHINGED TIMELINE of Boris Johnson, PM. For complicated administrative reasons, let us adhere to the notion that this is a work of fiction. Let us fight parody with truth, and truth with parody, on the understanding that all truth is in a sense parodic, and all parody essentially truthful.

*These passages of Unhinged Truth have been generated by artificial intelligence. A large learning model – AlgoPops Nut-Nut Beta Version 1.0 – has been given all available material concerning Boris Johnson and instructed to create a plausible analogue timeline in his voice, free from any legal unpleasantness.

July 2019

Discredited Narrative: Prime Minister Theresa May resigns after struggling to get parliamentary support for the Brexit deal she agreed with the European Union, which is then rejected three times by Parliament. Boris Johnson says he wants to replace her. US President Donald Trump endorses him. There is then a two-way contest between Johnson and Jeremy Hunt. Johnson is appointed prime minister and promises that Britain will leave the EU on 31st October, with or without a deal.

Unhinged Truth: I, Boris Johnson, Theresa May's most loyal supporter, plead with her to stay on and offer to 'strike with force any blackguard fomenting treason.' It was to no avail. '*Vulgus irata praevaluit…*' I write in my diary, my forehead pedimented with regret, one eyebrow raised into a Gothic arch of solemn determination. The angry mob has prevailed. 'This minority government must NOT be allowed to sink. No, it shall rise again!' Already the country is keening for me to Get Brexit Sorted. President Trump makes a secret visit to address the 1922 Committee by candlelight and says: 'This guy, Bosco Jackson, a beautiful singer. And he would make a great, great, great leader. Ass like a buffalo. Make him

Brexit King or just shoot yourselves in the fucking balls. Who's hungry?' A great cheer goes up and I accept the nomination (incidentally, narrowly avoiding a hammer attack by my rival, Jeremy Hunt – already a term of rhyming slang in the Members' Tea Room). That evening, I am lofted onto the shoulders of adoring ordinary folk and, under the close supervision of Special Branch operatives, paraded up and down Whitehall to the chants of happy Brits: 'Fuck you, Europe! Up the arse!'

August 2019

Discredited Narrative: Boris Johnson asks the Queen to prorogue Parliament from 10th September, thus reducing the time in which Parliament could block a no-deal Brexit.

Unhinged Truth: It would have been a terrible breach of royal protocol to reveal the details of any meeting with the fading yet doughty Queen while she was alive. Alas, she is no longer with us; only now may the truth be unhinged. I was summoned to Balmoral for a private audience with the monarch, in the legendary pantry where she would famously eat all her meals from Tupperware boxes. She removed her spectacles, took my hand (Great British strength still, in those majestic arms) and gazed at the microwave as if foreseeing a national destiny. What a presence. Boudicca in a twinset. 'Bobo,' she said (her private name for me ever since that bonkers night at Buck Pal, everyone pissed and playing Twister, or Pisster, as we called it!). 'Bobo, promise me you'll do everything in your power to throw off the yoke of tyrannical Europe, and let my people go!' I cannot tell a lie; I was deeply moved. I tried several times to take my leave, but dear Lillet (my private name for her, although I never used it in her company due to the enormous respect I had for her) wouldn't hear of it.

We stayed up all night singing old Cockney songs and dreaming of Britain as a revived naval superpower. 'Any old iron, any old iron' we sang, as rosy-fingered dawn spread herself against the window. 'Any, any, any old iron…' I felt the future throbbing within me. God bless her. And God bless the United Kingdom.

September 2019

Discredited Narrative: The prorogation of Parliament is ruled unlawful by the Supreme Court on 24th September. Boris Johnson denies lying to the Queen. His own brother, Jo, resigns from the Cabinet, unable to support the plans for a hard Brexit. The whip is withdrawn from 21 Conservative MPs for voting with an opposition motion on the issue. Amber Rudd resigns as Secretary of State for Work and Pensions. The Conservative government is left without a working majority in the Commons. The prime minister calls a general election for December.

Unhinged Truth: The Supreme Court has always resented me. I'm better looking and clearly more sexually active than any of them. And what in the name of gurgling fucking bollocks does 'unlawful' mean anyway? I'll tell you: it means 'Yah boo Boris, we hate you. Stick this up your bumhole.' Unlawful? Hello, I'm PRIME MINISTER. I AM the law. On top of it all, Amber quits in a huff (don't let the door hit your arse on the way out) and then my own bloody brother! Jo's always resented me. I'm better looking, et cetera. The withdrawal of the whip was supposed to be a '*pour encourager les autres*' thing, not a starting pistol for a sodding rebellion. They leave me with no choice. A general election it is. And let's see who gets more media coverage, shall we? Me, Labour's rag-tag battalion of Marxist vegetable growers, or the snivelling soft-Brexit bedwetters…

October 2019

Discredited Narrative: Boris Johnson publishes his Brexit plan, which includes a complicated arrangement for Northern Ireland. An amendment by Parliament delays Brexit until 31st January 2020. Downing Street confirms that Johnson will send a letter to the EU requesting an extension to Article 50 but will not sign it.

Unhinged Truth: So bored with Brexit. God. Let's get it done, as the late great Marvin Gaye once sang. Try to understand the Northern Ireland stuff, but apart from 'there will be no customs border in the Irish Sea, it would just float away in a high wind', it's all utterly baffling. Send a mocking note to the EU, ending 'yours petulantly', but don't sign it as a little, niggly extra dig. Quite like this. Propose to send unsigned letters to everyone from now on, to keep them on their toes. 'To all Chiefs of Staff. Prepare for nuclear war with Venezuela, signed ???' Ha ha ha! I bloody LOVE being prime minister!

November 2019

Discredited Narrative: Boris Johnson and Labour leader Jeremy Corbyn appear on ITV in a head-to-head election debate. The Conservative Party rebadges its Twitter account FactCheckUK and live-posts challenges to Corbyn's claims. The Electoral Commission condemns the subterfuge.

Unhinged Truth: Absolutely wiped the floor with Allotment Lenin. In a way, I wish it had been a fairer, more equal fight. In the blue corner, your trustworthy narrator – young, sexually active, charming, attractive, cultured, proud yet humble. In the red corner, a bearded gremlin – voice like an answerphone and an ideology smelling of mothballs and boiled cabbage. This is the dawning of the Age of Aquarius, I am the cup-bearer and it's full of a frisky malbec. Yeah, down the hatch baby. Sling your hook, Corbyn, and take your crappy bottle of Lucozade with you!

December 2019

Discredited Narrative: The decision to hold a snap general election brings a decisive victory for Boris Johnson: an 80-seat Conservative majority. Now the prime minister is able to force through a hard Brexit. Newly engaged to Carrie Symonds, he re-enters Number 10 with a hefty mandate.

Unhinged Truth: I knew instinctively what the British people wanted to see. They wanted to see a wall of polystyrene bricks with GRIDLOCK emblazoned across it, then me lurching through it on a digger with 'Get Bloody Brexit Sorted' stuck on the scoopy bit at the front. Couldn't have felt more like Achilles in a hard hat unless I'd tied Corbyn's corpse behind me and done a victory lap. As for Europe... Alas, soon a roaring sea and many metaphorical mountains will lie between us. I regret it has come to this. I am at heart a Europhile. I bloody love scoffing croissants, knocking back *le beaujolais nouveau* and fondling busty European women. But there's definitely more to be gained by leaving Europe. All sorts of treats are flooding in – free holidays and whatnot (some, ironically, in Europe). A nice rebalancing there. Told Carrie to order that gold wallpaper she fancies – don't worry about who'll pay for it. I'm bloody Achilles. Get yer knickers off, I'm about to enter Troy! Quick nip up to Balmoral where Her Royal Majesty greeted me in her wonderful Pearly Queen outfit. Offered me the PM gig, again. Roll out the barrel!

January 2020

Discredited Narrative: The United Kingdom formally leaves the European Union. Those opposed to Brexit warn that the UK economy will take a hit.

Unhinged Truth: 2020's going to be a fantastic year. Now we're pulling out of Europe, the economy will be tearing along the fast lane, soft top down, 'Start Me Up' by the Rolling Stones blaring out, a comely wench in a mini-skirt with – phwoar! – very squeezable thighs in the passenger seat. Literally the only thing that could sink my plan for an economic megaboost would be, I don't know, some sort of pandemic. And nobody's mentioned anything about that yet, as far as I know. At least I have recorded that nobody's mentioned it here, in my diary, on 5th January 2020. Although I shall, of course, be ultra vigilant… I address the nation and tell them we are at the dawn of a new era, when we'll really begin to unite, and level up, and spread hope and opportunity to every part of the UK, et cetera. Honestly, I've got a more or less permanent semi these days.

February 2020

Discredited Narrative: COVID-19 reaches the UK. By the end of the month there are 23 cases. There's a Cabinet reshuffle: Boris Johnson sacks five ministers and appoints Rishi Sunak as the Chancellor of the Exchequer.

Unhinged Truth: I'm obviously a little concerned about the threat from this coronavirus. A worryingly rapid viral spread eastward, the sort that Comrade Trotsky could only dream of. I summon Health Secretary Matt Hancock, eventually – he always seems to be in a closed session with one of his special advisers. As he tucks in his shirt and adjusts his tie, I outline my anxieties about COVID-19. He tells me it's just 'a flu-type thing, chillax.' I'm not so sure. I convene a meeting of COBRA to express my concern and ask that emergency procedures be put in place and ready to go at the drop of a hat. I don't want to cause panic, so I order that the COBRA meeting is to be super-secret, completely off the record, so that if anyone asks whether there *was* a COBRA meeting in a few years, at an inquiry say, everyone will have to be brave and say no.

March 2020

Discredited Narrative: The coronavirus pandemic hits the UK with full force, causing widespread panic. Boris Johnson is criticised for failing to attend COBRA briefings, for being unprepared and slow to act. He announces a nationwide lockdown, but later than most other countries and contributing to a subsequently high UK death toll. Public health messaging and an ineffective test-and-trace system are criticised. Sunak announces a £30 billion fund to protect the economy, £330 billion in business loan guarantees and a furlough scheme that would eventually cost £70 billion. Schools are shut, followed by pretty much everything else. Boris Johnson warns that 'tougher measures' may be introduced if people do not follow government advice on social distancing. He is seen publicly shaking hands with people, including hospital patients, on the same day the Scientific Advisory Group for Emergencies (SAGE) advises the public to minimise physical contact. Four days later he tests positive for the virus.

Unhinged Truth: Have absolutely loads more secret COBRA meetings that people won't find out about until now, in this sentence. With great reluctance, and against the official advice of government experts whose identity I must protect, I order a lockdown. There are already sniping, unpatriotic noises off about how the political class always looks out for themselves and their chums. I mean, come on. We're chucking around hundreds of billions of pounds, there's enough there for everyone to grab a fistful. I couldn't bear though to be thought a coward, hiding away at Number 10, miles away from the front line like a quivering conchie. No, I determine that I should contract this blasted virus and – *praesis ut prosis* – show leadership through service by then recovering from it. Abracadabra! Hey presto! *Pro bono publico*! I go around shaking hands with as many germy-looking proles as I can, even sneaking into a hospital's isolation ward and deliberately hugging the patients there, who are extremely shocked and delighted to see me!

April 2020

Discredited Narrative: Boris Johnson is taken to hospital, where he is quickly transferred to intensive care. He survives. Sir Keir Starmer is elected leader of the Labour Party, replacing Jeremy Corbyn. The Queen addresses the nation. NHS workers report the continuing lack of appropriate Personal Protective Equipment (PPE).

Unhinged Truth: The old corona knocked me out, but not for the count! I get myself up from the canvas, refocus – whammo-blammo! I return the compliment – KO! I stand over my felled opponent. I'm Muhammad Ali, all scowling in my gumshield. I dance around the ring, Hercules in boxing shorts. All credit to my constitution, which is like unto an ox, with the heart of a lion. Thanks also to the *Daily Mail*, who organised a Pray For Boris campaign, and to the Great British public. Recovering in my private ward, trying to work when possible, one night at 8 pm I hear their applause, their banging of saucepans and whatnot, a cacophony of heartfelt sympathy and support. This Get Well Soon Boris saucepan-banging is happening every week, I'm told. I am *loved*. I need specifically to thank the two nurses who helped save my life. Both immigrants, so there's a nice little sub-story there. We may not all of us necessarily approve of immigrants, but the ones who work in the NHS, scurrying about bravely in their improvised binbag costumes and ill-fitting facemasks, certainly get a thumbs-up from yours truly. As a precaution, I ask the Home Office to make sure their paperwork is in order.

May 2020

Discredited Narrative: COVID-19 now accounts for more than a quarter of all deaths in England and Wales. Boris Johnson and Carrie Symonds are married. Johnson comes under pressure to sack his senior adviser, Dominic Cummings, who broke lockdown rules by driving to Durham to self-isolate and then driving to Barnard Castle to 'test his eyesight'. A 'fast lane' for the procurement of government PPE contracts is set up, bypassing the usual tendering systems.

Unhinged Truth: Contrary to certain mischievous reports that I was 'relaxed about care home deaths as, let's face it, they're basically waiting rooms for the inevitable anyway', I am *extremely* concerned about the deaths of elderly people, who, like the redoubtable Captain Tom, are capable of raising huge amounts of money. I'm now a married man, so any extra-curricular hanky-panky is definitely off limits, you can take my word for that. Terrible fuss about Dom, let's hope at least some of it is untrue. Great to see some old pals (Jimbo, Shaggers, Wonky, et al) rolling up their sleeves for Britain and swinging some fantastic binbag deals for everyone.

June 2020

Discredited Narrative: Matt Hancock announces trials of a promising vaccine.

Unhinged Truth: I attend a Zoom meeting with senior NHS officials, who implore me to allow any successful COVID vaccine to be called the 'Boris Jab'. Absolutely not, we're all in this together, I tell them. Although, as we're about to sign off, it occurs to me that, if we WERE to name the vaccine – and nothing could be further from one's mind of course, the scientists and hedge fund guys who produced this 'Boris's Marvellous Medicine' as I hear some people might be calling it, they're the real heroes of the story – perhaps the 'Johnson Jab' might pack a real alliterative PUNCH? If everyone INSISTED on the Boris brand, perhaps the 'Boris Booster' as a sequel? 'Johnson', 'Boris', the old one-two. I see the little squares with faces in have all disappeared, but I commit these thoughts to the Zoom recording anyway. NICKNAMES got us through the Second World War, they'll get us through this shit-show. Thought: get Eric Clapton or that ginger bloke with the wide face everyone loves so much to re-record 'My Sharona' as 'Bye Corona'? Rallying cry, death to this new germ army!

July–September 2020

Holiday.

October 2020

Discredited Narrative: Boris Johnson resists the call from SAGE for a second lockdown. He's later reported as saying that Britain should just push through: 'Let the bodies pile high.' But with COVID deaths rising steeply again, Johnson announces a second lockdown, from the end of the month until 2nd December.

Unhinged Truth: To lockdown or not to lockdown, that is the question. Whether 'tis nobler in the mind to suffer the slings and arrows of outrageous fortune, honk honk, forsooth. SAGE are whining for another mass house arrest, but I have to weigh things very carefully. At Cabinet, I warn that the wrong decision could cost British lives – the greatest and most valuable of all lives – and that we would have to live with the moral consequences. 'Let the bodies pile high *in our consciences* if we get this wrong!' I say very carefully, clenching my fist, jaw, buttocks and balls to reinforce the point. Although no doubt this will be taken out of context, truncated and weaponised against me in the future. Ah well, so be it. I'm the boss. Them's the breaks.

November 2020

Discredited Narrative: The UK records the highest daily increase in COVID cases since mass testing began. A report by the National Audit Office found that suppliers of PPE with political connections were 10 times more likely to be awarded government contracts. The total spent on the NHS Test and Trace Programme reaches £22 billion, with some controversy over how the money has been spent and how effective it is.

Unhinged Truth: The usual moaners BLEATING on about how quickly this government's friends rushed to Britain's aid in its Second Darkest Hour. Some people simply can't bear to see a profit-driven private sector do what it does best. Working late into the night at Number 10 with a fortifying COCOA, I think I hear (horror!) some sort of social occasion underway downstairs. Right, let's see about this. I thunder down the stairs, listen very carefully, not a peep. Must have been the telly in the Spads' Common Room. Let's hope there wasn't even the slightest loosening of protocols, because I'll tell you who'll get it in the neck – MUGGINS here. I pad stealthily back to my study, thinking – not for the first time – *salus populi suprema lex esto*. Whatever laws are in place (and I should know, I AM fucking PRIME MINISTER) the welfare of the people, yes, THAT is the highest law. I will not cease from MENTAL fight, nor shall my sword sleep in my hand. Talking of which, feel the old sap rising again. Embarrassing really. Carrie says when it's sticking out of my polka-dot pyjamas, I look like a Dalek. Still, these are actually very serious times.

December 2020

Discredited Narrative: The government announces that families will be able to mix over the Christmas period. Throughout December, COVID cases rise significantly across the UK as a new, highly contagious variant surges through the population. On 21st December Boris Johnson announces tighter restrictions on mixing during Christmas and is heavily criticised for the late decision. Vaccinations begin.

Unhinged Truth: I know it comes with the territory, but I wish people would stop having a go all the fucking time, frankly. As I never tire of saying, I don't MAKE the rules, I simply delay them! Absolutely stonking Christmas though. Saw some lovely folk, drank too much, ate too much, danced too much, collided with furniture too much. Oh, all in a sensible, socially distanced way, of course. And to be honest, Party Animal Boris only lasted five minutes – I was absolutely back in my study straight after the Queen's Speech and hard at work, personally packing AstraZeneca vaccine jabs into boxes, sleeves rolled up and going at it like Comrade Stakhanov, but with much better hair and a top-notch education. Never mind your Soviet Five-Year Plans, I'll be here into my SEVENTIES,

I reckon. The most famous Johnson in the family by a mile, so massive tits and balls to YOU pater, I nearly wrote, then thought better of it. Yeah, tits and balls to ALL of you.

January 2021

Discredited Narrative: A third lockdown is announced after a record number of infections and deaths. Boris Johnson said he was 'deeply sorry' as the UK's COVID-related deaths pass the 100,000 mark, the first European country to do so.

Unhinged Truth: COVID… Yada yada, pina colada, of course YES, I mean it goes without saying, I'm 'deeply sorry' about any single death from the virus. In theory. Not sure how notionally multiplying that 'depth of sorrow' by 100,000 helps anyone, least of all the single death I was sorry about at the beginning of all this. Or have we simply forgotten all about him? Or possibly 'her' – it's always quite difficult identifying the first casualty in the fog of war. In any case, RIP, our thoughts are with you sir, or ma'am.

March 2021

Discredited Narrative: The government acknowledges the heroic efforts of NHS workers in what has been the most severe challenge since its creation. It pays tribute to those who worked 72-hour shifts in distressing circumstances, and honours the many frontline workers who lost their lives. It then offers NHS staff a 1% pay rise.

Unhinged Truth: Nobody loves the NHS more than I. It saved my life, in the name of Zeus! I have moved heaven and earth to get the Treasury to agree a pay rise for NHS workers. Would I have liked it to be more generous than 1%? Yes. Can we afford to give them more? No. Is that because we are absolutely broke having given all available money to Jimbo, Shaggers, Wonky, et al? Yes. Have we vaccinated half the country already, twice? Yes. Did we – well, most of us – clap for the NHS every week? Yes. Are MPs, members of the Cabinet and so on, pushing for a 1% pay rise from their various outside interests? That's none of my business. The world simply doesn't work like that, I'm afraid.

April 2021

Discredited Narrative: The funeral of Prince Philip, Duke of Edinburgh takes place at Windsor Castle. COVID restrictions mean there is a limit of 30 guests. An iconic photograph of the Queen, masked and alone in a pew, will later be collated with images of partying at Downing Street taken at the same time. Dominic Cummings, having finally been sacked, alleges that Boris Johnson arranged for Tory donors to secretly pay for lavish renovations at Number 11 Downing Street. In the Commons, Sir Keir Starmer asked who had paid for the redecoration. Johnson said he had. He hadn't. The money came from a donor.

Unhinged Truth: 17th April. Very sad day. The funeral of Prince Philip. I wish most fervently I could have been there to pay my respects. He had a profound influence on my own hilarious-but-never-racist takes on overseas folk. Oh, he could sound off-hand sometimes, with his old-fashioned terms – like 'picaninnies with watermelon smiles', which many people attribute to me when, in fact, I borrowed the phrase from HRH PP, and IRONISED it. I stand alone in my office as night falls, raising a glass to the grand old duke. I just hope the official photographer who took the shot doesn't let it out of his sight. For all I know, some giggling political mischief-maker (e.g. Dom) might have it photoshopped into what looks like a party scenario at Number 10. Here's to you, Phil. Thanks for all the laughs that really weren't slurs at all. Goodnight sweet prince. And now back to the important documents I'm dealing with, and trying to ignore the noisy distraction of who paid for the fucking wallpaper. Please, Prince Philip is dead, show a little respect.

May 2021

Discredited Narrative: The Conservatives gain ground against Labour in local by-elections, including the previously safe Labour stronghold of Hartlepool. Around one million people have been given leave to work from home indefinitely. Boris Johnson confirms that an independent inquiry into the government's handling of the COVID crisis will begin in spring 2022. Dominic Cummings gives evidence to MPs, claiming that tens of thousands of people died unnecessarily because of government mistakes, that Johnson ignored scientific advice, delayed imposing lockdowns and is 'unfit for the job'. He also says that health secretary Matt Hancock should have been removed from office for lying about protecting care homes from COVID.

Unhinged Truth: '*Fas est ab hoste doceri*', as Ovid said. One may learn even from one's enemies. Sad to see a once-good friend turn into a treacherous bastard who has now got it in not just for me but also for my family. I am apparently The Trolley, Carrie is Princess Nut-Nut, and my father Stanley is The Wife-Beating Shitbag. It is intolerable. I think Dom's gone seriously mad, eyes popping out of his lightbulb bonce and compelled to gabble a hateful stream of consciousness. It's all nonsense, of course. I have never,

EVER ignored scientific advice – I simply haven't had the time to read it. And I think the British people are sensible enough to work out who killed their nearest and dearest. Was it 'government mistakes', Dom, or the COVID-19 virus? You tell me! Some fantastic beams of sunlight are piercing the gloom though. We got Hartlepool. Weird place somewhere in the North, where they hanged a monkey in the early nineteenth century thinking it was a French spy. That's the North for you. Levelling up? Of course. Primate murder? No thanks. Anyway, the point is it's been solid Labour since the monkey business. All those years they apparently didn't even bother to count the Labour votes, they just WEIGHED them. Now it's swung to us. Or to ME, let's face it. Also, the *Sunday Times* Rich List has been published. Incredible! The wealth of the UK's billionaires increased by 21.7% during COVID to £597.2 billion and we now have a record 171 of the lucky bastards. About time I went for drinks with Jimbo, Shaggers and Wonky...

July 2021

Discredited Narrative: Boris Johnson announces that most generalised health restrictions are to be replaced by recommendations.

Unhinged Truth: We're out of the woods, we're gambolling through the meadow and the sun is shining. Instruct the comms team to set up an 'out of office' message on the email. Funny old phrase, isn't it? 'Out of office'.

August 2021

Holiday.

September 2021

Discredited Narrative: A fuel crisis hits the country, caused by supply chain issues. Due to ensuing panic buying, many petrol stations run dry. There's widespread disapproval after a photo of the Cabinet shows 'at least 30 people crammed shoulder to shoulder' with nobody wearing a face mask and all windows shut, contrary to the government's own advice.

Unhinged Truth: I'm not really one for conspiracy theories – no gunman on the grassy knoll, definitely a moon landing or two, COVID not spread by 5G masts – but this fuel crisis sounds a bit *voidy* when you give it a knock, *n'est-ce pas?* I mean, yah, those shoppers who aggressively bundled a metric tonne of bog roll into their trolleys last year are exactly the sort to queue for hours at the local BP to squeeze a fiver's worth of unleaded in their tiny cars, having BURPED out a fiver's worth in exhaust fumes. On the other hand, isn't this so-called fuel crisis *precisely* the sort of doomsday scenario that gives the Remoaners a hard-on? Honestly, I think some people have never fully recovered from their slo-mo COVID panic attacks. They need a crisis to make their lives whole again. All this fuss over the unmasked Cabinet. Come on guys, we're leading the country back to the elevated plateau of contentment, the *sole perfunditur*, all hunkering down and getting on with the job. Some people just love DRAMA. So, we were close together, so what? That's how politics works! What next, masks on in a fucking rugby scrum? Nonsense.

October 2021

Discredited Narrative: Addressing the Conservative Party Conference, the prime minister sets out his plans for uniting and levelling up the country: 'Build Back Better'. Boris Johnson praises capitalism and wealth creation, crediting the former with developing a vaccine. The British Medical Association accuses the government of being 'wilfully negligent' for not reimposing mandatory face masks. The number of daily COVID infections exceeds 50,000 for the first time since July.

Unhinged Truth: Absolutely bloody stormed Conference. I'm Thatcher in trousers. Heseltine with a swingier dick. 'Build Back Better' – what a fantastic phrase. It's exactly this kind of cleverness, alliteration and wordplay that puts the Tory party right up there, Beatles level, while Starmer and his miserabilist rabble in their jumble sale clothes are the Dave Clark Five, or whoever. With a push and a shove, come 2024, that'll be the number of MPs they have too: FIVE. Fuck me though, the culture wars stuff really gets Conference wet. And it costs nothing. You simply have to stand up there, jowls wobbling, claiming the humourless she/hers and he/hims and the er, er, she/hims – whatever, that lot, you don't even need to think it through – they really do want to rewrite our national story, starting with Hereward the Woke. God, I am a political colossus (even though Carrie keeps on and on at me to lay off the carbs for a bit, 'like being trapped under a bloody Victorian wardrobe'.) Hereward the WOKE, though, honk honk! *Veni* (to Manchester, no idea it was this far away), *vidi* (don't know what's uglier, the urban hellscape or its rat-faced inhabitants who've walked straight out of a Lowry painting but wearing knock-off designer leisure-wear), *vici* (still, mostly indoors with My People, who all want to touch my robe). Yeah, motherfuckers. Behold Alexander Boris de Pfeffel CAESAR!

November 2021

Discredited Narrative: A new COVID variant, Omicron, is identified. Face coverings again become compulsory on public transport and in shops. Boris Johnson is photographed without a face mask during a visit to a hospital. Meanwhile, he backs a motion to block the suspension of Tory MP Owen Paterson, found to have abused his government position by lobbying for a company he was a consultant for. Instead, Johnson wants the creation of a new committee to examine reforms. Thirteen MPs defy the three-line whip and vote against. Opposition parties say they will boycott any such committee. A media backlash is followed by Paterson's resignation. Inflation hits 4.2%, the highest for 10 years.

Unhinged Truth: Thanks a bunch, inflation. As if I haven't got enough on my wholly inadequate fucking plate. This Paterson kerfuffle has taken a bit of the shine off my imperial reign, I must say. Oh and of course my loyal tenure as the nation's most humble servant, obviously. Pissed off at OP, tbqfhwy. On the plus side, he did nothing wrong, unless we apply a ridiculously old-fashioned moral template. On the minus, he was found out, quite the worst thing that can happen. Makes one look GUILTY. An awful lot of awful people getting on their awfully high horses about this, as if anyone in life might be said to be entirely blameless. Why on earth do people keep scuttling up to me and bothering me about 'parties' at Number 10? I'm writing this on 26th November 2021, by the way, just so there's no confusion. As far as I know, the COVID rules and regulations have been followed to the LETTER here at Number 10 Downing Street. (Diary entry, 26-11-21, witnessed by SIR Gavin Williamson and others.)

December 2021

Discredited Narrative: More stringent COVID restrictions for England are announced and lead to the largest Tory rebellion so far. Revelations start to emerge about several illegal parties held in Downing Street. The growing scandal is called 'Partygate'. A leaked video shows advisers apparently joking about a recent party at Number 10. The sole woman involved – press secretary Allegra Stratton – is the only one to resign. Boris Johnson apologises. Labour calls for Johnson to resign if he misled Parliament. A photograph is published by the *Daily Mirror* of Johnson at a quiz night. Senior civil servant Simon Case recuses himself from leading an inquiry into Partygate after reports that a similar event was held in his own office. The *Guardian* publishes a photo of Boris Johnson, his wife and 17 staff members in the Downing Street garden enjoying cheese and wine, at a time when large social gatherings were prohibited.

Unhinged Truth: Yeah, Merry Fucking Christmas. Has anyone anywhere ever been lumbered with such useless subordinates? I am as SHOCKED as anyone to hear that I may inadvertently have attended social gatherings at Number 10. How shocked? Well, I've adjusted my 'shocked face' in the mirror this morning, turned it right up to 11, and let me tell you, it looks bloody scary. I mean properly, properly 'late-night horror film at that old fleapit in Oxford, back row, blowie from some Sloaney stargazer' shocked. I completely, COMPLETELY understand the feelings of the relatives of those who died frightened and alone in hospital while allegedly some arsehole downstairs here was careening around to Whitney Houston. It breaks my heart. It does. If I discover that one of my staff actually did that – God forbid – I swear I'll be like the character Jules in *Pulp Fiction*. I will strike down upon them with great VENGEANCE and furious anger, et cetera. Even the thought is unacceptable. Unacceptable. Fuck, let's hope next year's better. While I breathe, I hope. *Dum spiro spero. Que sera sera.* No no, no no no no, no no no no, no no, there's no limit. Grr, come on 2022, I am DONE with 2021, bitch.

January 2022

Discredited Narrative: An ITV news report reveals more details of the May 2020 garden party. Boris Johnson apologises in the Commons for attending, saying he believed it was a 'work event'. Critics point out that such a thing was in any case banned under COVID regulations. Senior civil servant Sue Gray will report. David Davis MP calls for Johnson to resign. Johnson blames Starmer for the non-prosecution of serial rapist and necrophile Jimmy Savile. The Metropolitan Police contacts the government over widespread reports of COVID rule breaches, including an email inviting 100 people to a 'bring-your-own-booze' event in the Downing Street garden during the first lockdown. The High Court rules the government's use of a 'VIP lane' to award contracts for PPE to two companies was unlawful. Johnson confirms he did attend a party in the Downing Street garden during the first lockdown in May 2020 and offers his 'heartfelt apology'. Allegations of serial rule-breaking at Number 10 start to pile high.

Unhinged Truth: The performative fuss people make over every little imagined misdemeanour. Look, I stand by my comments about Starmer and Jimmy Savile, such as they are. I said Starmer hadn't prosecuted Savile, and he hadn't. Neither had I, nor had any ordained member of the Anglican church, nor any member of an Olympic bobsleigh team. Who cares? Calm down everyone. What a confected syllabub of PIDDLE. I hate it when my easy-going charm and laissez-faire attitude is weaponised against me. Sometimes one wonders if people are deliberately taking everything I say out of context just so they can think themselves clever. Work events two YEARS ago? The world has moved on a bit since then, chum. Is it healthy, all this trawling the past? God, to think last year they may have erected a statue of me... How did Pericles put it? 'What you leave behind is not what is engraved in stone monuments, but what is woven into the lives of others.' Yes, well, I wish some of those raking over the ashes of the past would remember the GETTING BLOODY BREXIT DONE. AND the vaccine roll-out. Now THERE was something woven into bloody people's lives. I was fucking King Jab. I was fucking Antidote Father Christmas! *Eheu.* Alas. Life goes on. Tell you what does give me the horn – meeting Meghan Markle at a formal event, ideally a funeral. When you get close up, she smells of gardenias.

February 2022

Discredited Narrative: Munira Mirza resigns as Director of the Number 10 Policy Unit, in protest at Boris Johnson's Starmer/Savile remarks. Three further senior aides resign hours later. More photographic evidence of Partygate emerges. The Queen tests positive for COVID.

Unhinged Truth: I don't mind admitting I needed that. An adoring public once again cheering me through the streets. 'Bo-ris! Bo-ris!' Yeah, baby. I'm Churchill. I'm Augustus. I am BORIS. There's only one Boris in the media and name recognition is everything, isn't it? Yes, 'Prime Minister Boris Johnson' but beyond that: 'Brand Boris.' The Cabinet all stand when I enter the room, applauding me. An old woman in the street offers me a rose. What a day. I have to catch a plane home, but seriously Ukraine, it's been real. I'll be back soon, President Zelenskyy. Back where I'm bloody well appreciated.

March 2022

Discredited Narrative: Nazanin Zaghari-Ratcliffe, detained by Iran in 2016, is freed and allowed to return to the UK. Boris Johnson's critics question why it took so long to secure her release. As foreign secretary, Johnson erroneously said she had been training journalists there. P&O Ferries sacks 800 employees via a video call, saying they are to be replaced by cheaper agency staff, prompting outrage. The Met announces that 20 fixed penalty notices will be issued as part of the Partygate inquiry.

Unhinged Truth: Tremendous news that Nazareth Thingummy-Wotsit has been freed, you'd *think*. But it hasn't moved my bloody personal approval ratings up by a single sodding percentage point. *Au contraire*. Dropped in on the new spads who've replaced the ones who quit. Caught one of them telling the others that something or other was 'total chaos' as I galloped in clutching my World's Best Boss mug. Everyone looking guilty. Not having it. Politics is a tug of war. Everyone pulls hard or you get fucking P&O'd.

April 2022

Discredited Narrative: The price cap for gas and electricity rises by 54%. Boris Johnson and Rishi Sunak are among those issued with a Fixed Penalty Notice for Partygate breaches. Johnson becomes the first sitting prime minister to be sanctioned for breaking the law. He apologises to the House of Commons, saying he didn't realise he had breached rules at the time. Tory MP Neil Parish admits to watching pornography twice in the House of Commons and says that he will resign as an MP.

Unhinged Truth: People complaining about their gas bills going up. Blame Putin, not me. Oh, and all this fluff about a piddling little fine. It's a Fixed Penalty. It's like four points on my prime minister's leadership licence. Let he who is without a speeding fine cast the first stone. It's not like I watched indecent matter in the House. I mean, what was Parish thinking? I remember when they allowed cameras in the chamber for the first time in the late 80s – would it somehow besmirch the dignity of Parliament, et cetera. Fuck me, if Margaret Thatcher could have seen where it would all lead – a Tory MP not merely disconnected from proceedings, but consuming Sodom and GOMORRAH on a portable telephone connected to something called the internet – she'd think the world had gone mad. We live in volatile times. *O tempora! O mores!* Every morning there's a new story about some CHUMP getting caught for unsolicited fondling, arse-slapping, non-sanctioned fumblings-about. That sort of thing goes on all the time, of course, but not as a shitting *Times* exclusive, you careless berks. Please, I beg you, my Conservative foot soldiers. Observe my Three Rules for Public Life: discipline, temperance, caution. Onward!

May 2022

Discredited Narrative: Problems escalate for Boris Johnson as the Partygate scandal ratchets up and more details emerge of his botched attempt to save Owen Paterson. The war in Ukraine worsens. There is a deepening cost of living crisis. The Tories suffer widespread defeat in local council elections. Photographs obtained by ITV News show Johnson raising a glass at a leaving party inside Number 10. A number of MPs suggest he lied to the House of Commons.

Unhinged Truth: Time to circle the wagons, I tell my staunchest allies. The whooping, ululating, gurgling Native Americans surrounding us, on their horses supplied no doubt by Iran and with their rifles from North Korea, will surely fight to the death. Well, let me tell you, THIS paleface will never, ever give up! Cue huge, huge wave of applause and cheering. The simpering Labour party, I go on, now led by that awful chartered accountant, is coming for me. Indeed, some members of my own party have formed a sort of Vichy Labour cabal and plot my downfall. The ravenous media is bog-snorkelling through my recent history looking for incriminating bits of nonsense that they might glue together to 'prove' my guilt. Let them. I fear no one. Because I know that we valiant few, comrades and friends, will face the future together and triumph. Yeah, I'm back in Ukraine again.

June 2022

Discredited Narrative: The Queen's Platinum Jubilee concludes; it is clear she is not in good health. More than 50 Tory MPs submit letters calling for the removal of Boris Johnson as leader of the party; he survives a vote of no confidence by 211 to 148. Sex scandals and more Partygate revelations increase the pressure on him to stand down. Senior Tory Michael Howard calls on Johnson to resign. Oliver Dowden, party co-chairman, resigns. Johnson says he intends to stay on as prime minister until the mid-2030s. A statement from 10 Downing Street later makes it clear he was joking. Conservative Deputy Chief Whip Chris Pincher resigns; it's later alleged that he had sexually assaulted two men.

Unhinged Truth: All this noise. Such a relief to be up to Balmoral again. These days it makes a peaceful alternative to Kyiv. Lillet looking quite drawn, as if she's had quite enough of everything. I know how she feels. The temptation to just say fuck it, I've given it my all, the people love me, but like Coriolanus, I feel betrayal is always just *there*, just beside me, waiting to bite me in the balls. I congratulate HM on the great success of her Platty Joobs. She seems remote now, a little colder. I try to lighten the mood by saying 'Platty Joobs. Sounds like a 1970s porn mag!' She asks me if I'm going to resign. I tell her no. I'm a FIGHTER not a quitter. She says she's met a few people like me in the world of racing. Punters who can't leave it alone, who have to double down on a bad bet rather than get out before they lose their shirt. 'Escalation of commitment to a lost cause,' she says, sternly. I rather hope she's not suggesting I *am* that lost cause. She offers me a horrible, squashed grey vol-au-vent from a Tupperware box. I wordlessly refuse. She shrugs and gobbles it up herself. Crumbs everywhere. 'You know, Boris,' she says fondly, 'You're so very likeable and funny and clever, but I'm afraid you'll never be a great politician.' 'Oh, and why's that?' I ask, ready to leave. 'Because you're a terrible PERSON, Boris. You're an awful, awful BASTARD.' She turns away. Fucking hell, always the ones you least expect, isn't it? I think I prefer the House of Commons after all.

July 2022

Discredited Narrative: Boris Johnson tells the BBC he had been informed of a misconduct complaint against Chris Pincher before appointing him Deputy Chief Whip, admitting his decision was a 'bad mistake'. Dominic Cummings alleges Johnson joked that he was 'Pincher by name and pincher by nature.' Rishi Sunak and Sajid Javid resign. Over the next 24 hours more than 60 government officials also resign. Calls for Johnson to go rise to an unignorable clamour. Levelling up secretary Michael Gove refuses to affirm his support. Johnson sacks him, then resigns as prime minister.

Unhinged Truth: Mimsy Gove, that four-eyed fucking arsehole. Face like a MUDSKIPPER, stupid flapping girly hands, never trusted him. Well good luck now mate, enjoy your status as Boring Footnote in British Political History. Hey-ho, all things must pass, all flesh is grass, *quand c'est l'heure, c'est l'heure*... Once in every few generations, a beloved public figure must do the honourable thing for Queen and country and graciously retreat, for the good of all. Like Jesus, I must die for the sins of all mankind, however unfair and frankly fucking shitty that is. But fear not, for like Jesus, I shall return. Not just for a couple of days to dazzle everyone and then disappear upstairs, but for a long time. I'll just say this: many of those who brought about my downfall are clearly envious; although I am pushing 60, I am younger, better looking and more sexually active than any of them. I leave with my dignity and reputation INTACT. Might write a book.

Part Two

BE MORE BORIS

Boris Johnson's life is a masterclass in how to be ruthlessly ambitious yet in a humorous and endearing way. The occasional error of judgement, those moments when his exuberant enthusiasm for life perhaps leads him slightly astray, merely make him more human and relatable.

In the following pages we'll learn how to apply the lessons of Boris's life to our own. And as we saw with the great Get Brexit Done campaign, every course of self-improvement – whether national or individual – begins with a short, snappy slogan. That's why everyone can and should Be More Boris.

It's not simply a question of working out what it is you want, getting what you want, holding on to it with dwindling enthusiasm and then seeing something you want more and grasping for that instead. It's a completely different way of achieving your goals by using forward-thinking techniques.

So, how can we Be More Boris to achieve, modify or completely reimagine our life goals? Could Being More Boris bring both welcome order and mischievous chaos into our world at the same time? Might we even spread happiness to others by making our lives more self-centred and then, by Being More Boris, leave them with some curiously fond memories of our relationship?

Let's find out, as together we set off on our adventure at an exhilaratingly high speed. Destination: a More Boris You. Honk honk!

If It Ain't Fixed, Break It

Kintsugi Politics

Every prime minister wants to make their mark, to leave a legacy. In his three short years as PM – that actually felt very much longer – Boris Johnson perfected the art of what we might call 'Kintsugi Politics'.

Kintsugi is the Japanese art of repairing broken pottery with gold, silver or platinum. Something broken and repaired in this way becomes more precious than something that has never been broken. That's what Johnson, a political genius, did with politics. He smashed all the protocols he could find, especially those connected to public trust, and then put the pieces back together with pure gold, e.g. government contracts for party donors. He adopted an informal approach to decision-making, and flashy living. And it worked. Has trust in politicians ever been higher?

Be More Boris: Break things, mend things, so they're better than before. We can apply this basic principle every day to aspects of our own humdrum lives.

Free Time Is Me Time

How busy do people think you are? The gap between the number of hours a day you *actually* work and how many hours people *think* you work determines the amount of free time you have, theoretically. It's important to maintain a healthy work–life balance, and Boris Johnson is a master of time maintenance.

After his general election victory, Johnson stood outside Number 10 and promised he and his colleagues would 'work round the clock' to repay the trust of those who had voted Conservative for the first time.[1] Of course, that would be the easiest promise to break; nobody works 24 hours a day, not even a workaholic. And he'd seen too many political lives lost to the demon work; it wasn't going to happen to him. To those outside the giddy world of governance, the scheduling of afternoon naps, long quasi-official lunches and private social events may seem indulgent. It's not. It's kintsugi: break the day into pieces, then put the pieces back together with agreeably golden glue. It's simply a better day.

> Be More Boris: Give more time to yourself and less time to others. On the face of it, selfish. But this way, me-time becomes routine, and them-time more precious.

You finish the call and slump back into the sofa, idly scrolling through the endless mediocre streams of shit on the TV. Your partner comes in to remind you that you're taking your daughter to football training on Saturday morning. 'It's just I heard you on the phone talking about "brunch" with someone? Who has time for "brunch"?' 'Well,' you say airily, 'I do, actually. Been ages since I've seen Phil. Thought we could have a catch-up over a late breakfast, maybe go on for a few drinks and then a mate of his has got us tickets for a show. What?' You tell them they look as though they've just swallowed a guinea pig.

'But you *always* take her to football because I *always* have to work on Saturdays…' 'And that is your right,' you concede. 'It's your life, and you must live it as you wish, working on Saturdays if you must. I've simply decided to re-order my time to make it more valuable – not just for me, but for everyone. If I take her to football every Saturday, you and she see it as routine time. If, however, I take her once in an entire season, well. That's incredibly special.'

'Well, I can't take her!' 'God, calm down,' you say. 'We'll delegate. I'm sure she can cadge a lift with a friend.' Your partner's clearly disgruntled. 'We'll discuss this later. I'm running late as it is…' 'Yeah, not tonight,' you say. 'I saw you *last* night. I have a new and urgent priority in my life: me. You see, the reason I'm bored with…' – here you wave your arm around, indicating *everything* – 'all this, is because it's…' – here you pull a Noel Coward face – 'mundane. Quotidian. Dull, dull, dull, my dear.'

'You selfish arsehole,' observes your partner, not entirely unreasonably. 'You're leaving us?' 'Oh, no, no, no,' you say. 'I'm simply making family time *more* special by reducing the amount available. The way OPEC does with oil. Less family time equals more precious family time. In fact, I'm off down the pub. Fancy coming? Well, you can't. There. I've already *specialised* us.'

A month later you realise they've taken custody not only of your daughter but of the house, the car and the joint account. See? You were right. All that seems a lot more special now. Never mind. You know what's really special? You, and your you-time.

If It Ain't Broke, Brexit

The Brexit conducted by self-confessed Europhile Boris Johnson was a brilliant demonstration of how Kintsugi Politics works. Not only did it break the way Brexit had been imagined – an orderly, respectful separation from the European Union – but it broke the promise of what Brexit would bring to the UK. We're still in the process of putting the shattered pieces of our destiny back together, but we have already seen some surprising results. Johnson the great disruptor should be very proud of the far-reaching Brexit–Fixit consequences.

The smashing-up stage of Brexit went very well indeed, thanks to Boris and his chief adviser Dominic Cummings, five feet seven inches of unquenchable wrath in a hoodie. Cummings said he'd Get Brexit Done for Boris, but only if all the Downing Street special advisers reported directly to him.[2] It was a difficult decision for the prime minister, who'd hoped to do all the hard work himself, but he agreed for the sake of the country.

However, Brexit delivered something much more important: Britain's status as the most powerful country in the world. Boris had somehow not merely turned the clock back to 1945, when we'd defeated Hitler and saved the world, but to 1588 when an armada of European infamy had been sent packing the first time. Britain is now ascending to greatness under Charles III as it once did under Elizabeth I.

How the broken pieces of EU membership will finally be put back together to create a better, stronger, more independent Great Britain is irrelevant. After all, policies are abstract concepts. What our hero put together in the wake of Brexit was something real: a tingly sense inside all patriots that they were British, and therefore exceptional. Not just patriotism, but Kintsugi Patriotism.

Be More Boris: If you disrupt a long-term relationship, the pieces of you when re-assembled will feel renewed and exceptional.

You're waiting to see the doctor. You can't shift this chesty cough. You've been with this practice for 40 years, but you've felt restless lately. All these prescribed meds, the endless bossiness about diet and fitness, the nagging over the number of units consumed each week... They're simply bureaucratic diktats, aren't they? Oh, and your weight is in kilos these days, and your height is in metres.

You're called from the waiting room and follow the doctor in. Time to take back control! 'So, what seems to be the trouble?' she asks. 'Oh, nothing really. Mere bagatelle. Bit of a cough. Not quite ready to, er, er, pay Charon the ferryman to cross over into the unknown unknown *yet*, what what, pip pip, honk honk!' 'Right, well let's have a listen, shall we? If you can just take your shirt off…'

A line must be drawn. You fold your arms and refuse. 'But I need to listen to your chest.' You make it clear you're perfectly capable of hearing the drumbeat of your own chest. And that it is puffed out with, er, er, Great British Hyperbole! 'But you made an appointment to see someone about a possible chest infection?' 'The past is a foreign country,' you say. 'I have other patients to…' With respect, you'd like to finish your comment. You tell her your lungs have belted out 'Swing Low, Sweet Chariot' at Twickenham. They were clearly functioning perfectly well *then*.

The doctor asks if you're feeling OK 'in yourself'. You resent the implication and insist that 'in yourself' is exactly how you intend to live from now on. 'Well, if you really don't want me to examine you and you're feeling fine now, I suppose I'll wish you good luck and move on to my next patient. I'm already running half an hour late.'

You march over to the door, swing it open and address the waiting room. 'So much for improving NHS services under a Labour government! The conversation I've just had has included such irrelevant piffle-paffle as Ancient Greek funereal protocol and some wokery about internal feelings. It is a disgrace. I urge you all to leave.' The commotion has attracted another, bigger doctor who asks *you* to leave the surgery or calm down and talk things through. Or he will escalate the situation. You remove your shirt and adopt a fighting stance. 'Oh, allow *me* to escalate the situation! Put 'em up. Queensberry Rules, honk honk!'

Be sure to leave at this point. Doctors are famously in great shape, and there's no telling how have-a-go-hero your fellow patients might be feeling. Email the surgery later to explain your bizarre behaviour. You're experimenting with microdosing at the moment and took ten times the recommended hit. The surgery will totally understand and might well recommend a psych consultation. There, you've fixed things. The doctor–patient bond is stronger than ever. Your GP has seen worse mental health crises, and now you're very much in the system.

Except the police were alerted and came to your house. You ended up with a Fixed Penalty Notice and a fine for anti-social behaviour, and had your place turned over for drugs (let's hope they didn't find any). OK, perhaps you hadn't thought this through. You can't remember if anyone in the waiting room looked familiar, you've been put on an NHS security list and the surgery will in future try to keep you on telephone appointments only. Still, it's *fixed*. Hurrah for Borisivity!

Represent Others with your Happiness

Much of the wholly unwarranted abuse directed towards The People's Prime Minister concerned his alleged conduct during the lockdown periods of the COVID pandemic. Selflessly, he allowed a great deal of this abuse to be pushed through his personal letterbox. But hang on a moment… It's time for an 'unhinged' reappraisal.

Johnson's premiership coincided with the worst pandemic the world had seen for generations. To date, the deaths of over 230,000 British citizens have been related to COVID.[3] Those were dark days, indeed, and strange to remember. Lonely deaths in hospital, with family members denied contact. Schools closed, pubs locked up, businesses shuttered. Streets quiet apart from birdsong, in some weird reversal of Silent Spring.

Who could forget that iconic photograph of a solitary Queen at her husband's funeral?[4] Certainly not certain hypercritical members of the British public, who rather brutally contrasted Her Majesty's quiet, dignified grief with the raucous piss-ups at Number 10. 'One rule for us, another for them', the charge sheet read.

But the whole thing – wilful or not – is a complete misunderstanding. Kintsugi Politics required the prime minister to break the long-standing contract between the government and the public which held that everyone was 'in this thing together'. And then he had to fix it, to make it better *in the long run*. Perhaps it will take a generation to fully understand, but it will be understood. The Downing Street Pandemic Piss-Ups were a morale booster, a tonic for the nation, this century's version of those spirit-lifting lunchtime recitals of Bach given during World War Two by Dame Myra Hess at the National Gallery.

In a few decades' time, the country will look back on Partygate and see it for what it truly was – a defiant light in the gloom, a glow of bulldog spirit, wheeled clanking into the nation's HQ in a Samsonite travel case.[5] Johnson and his *actual* party members, the glorious few, were a sturdy home guard indeed, chasing away despair with mojitos and dispelling fear with karaoke. We shall remember them.

Be More Boris: Sometimes sacrifice means breaking the rules for the greater good. And sometimes sacrifice means being happy when others can't.

You're at the funeral of a cousin. You didn't know him that well, and it's been years since you've seen him. Turns out he was quite religious. The funeral service is taking place in a grand cathedral and there are aisles and aisles full of mourners. It's a very solemn vibe, people sniffling and sobbing, as if this is the darkest day since England lost in the 1996 Euros. Come on, everyone, get a grip, life goes on. Chumbawamba, man!

Interminable eulogies, one after the other from family members who can barely hold it together. Oh, fucking hell. Now the priest is on, talking about Saint Cousin's life of devotion and service to others. A lot of the material is familiar from the earlier eulogies, the youth work he did, turning countless young lives around. The OBE. The campaigning against poverty, I mean, come on, like anyone's going to campaign *for* it.

'He will be remembered by so many people,' drones the priest, 'for so many different acts of kindness, for all the singular ways he brought joy into our lives. I'm sure everyone here has a story, and I'm sure today we'll be hearing many of them.' And that's when you remember.

Years and years ago – must have been about eight, both of you – at a family wedding. Bored, cruising the half-empty tables while the grown-ups were dancing, you gulped down whatever alcohol you could find. A blurry memory of being out the back of wherever it was, counting up the money you'd both stolen from the jackets and handbags left unattended. Smoking your first cigarettes and starting to feel a bit ill. And then he puked. Little Saint Cousin OBE puked, then slipped in the vomit and just lay there on the ground crying. You honestly remember it as being one of the funniest things you've ever seen.

You're laughing now at the memory. And then you realise you've been on your feet addressing the whole congregation at high volume and now the ushers are gently removing you. But at least you shared this moment of happiness with so many people and must have brought some smiles to a few faces. It's what your cousin would have wanted.

Keep Pushing your Targets Forward

Boris Johnson pledged quite a few things at the start of his prime ministership. No, they weren't fulfilled, but something even better happened: they were broken and kintsugi'd to make the country even more aspirational.

There weren't as many police officers or nurses or GPs or houses as promised. The '40 new hospitals' he said would be built, for example, weren't technically *built*, but the idea of them was at least broken and put back together to mean something new.[6] A prefabricated cabin in a car park might be thought of as a new 'emergency wing' if that supported the narrative of national advancement, for example.

Imagine for a moment that those pledges had actually been met. Job done. What would then happen to the sense of a nation striving to be better? The pledges didn't fail, they were broken in order for national aspiration to continue to be a driving force in our great island story. Of course we're still desperately short of nurses, et cetera. We need them urgently. And that's aspirational Kintsugi Politics. You break the promise, put the promise back together, it's somehow an even better promise because you now need nurses even *more* urgently.

Be More Boris: Drive other people to being their aspirational best by deliberately breaking your promises, thus putting whatever they wanted further away, driving them on to even greater aspiration.

You don't even need to be out in the world breaking stuff to bring a little Kintsugi Boris into your life. Imagine you're reading a book. It's pretending to be one of those life-lesson jobs yet – preposterously – it's based on the career of Boris Johnson. You've got to the part where you're urged essentially to break shit, then fix shit, in order to improve shit? You may think your life doesn't need breaking and fixing, but you're wrong. And you're wrong because you're a fucking idiot. Hang on, is there some fourth-wall bollocks going on here?

Yes. There is. You were stupid enough initially when you bought this book. It's about Boris Johnson, so how 'good' did you 'think' it would be? You're additionally stupid – and I mean as thick as the earth's crust – to believe that any angle on the most morally absent prime minister in living memory would yield any useful guidance whatsoever. Please, nobody's interested in your thin, colourless life. At all. Go away and think about the crestfallen failure you truly are.

Wait, wait, come back. The paragraph above demonstrates how to break the trust between a reader and an author. It is, of course, quite shocking for anyone to do that, except as a demonstration of how kintsugi works. And this paragraph is all about putting the trust back together. Because we both know that one reason you bought this book is that you recognise sarcasm and understand how irony works. You think that Boris Johnson *thinks* he's clever because he can fool quite a lot of people, whereas you *are* clever because you think you can see through Boris

Johnson. This book clearly has a self-selecting readership of people who get what's going on here. You're brilliant, and I can only hope that you find it in your heart to forgive me.

Finding the pieces, refitting them, making the trust whole again. But even better now, because the trust is repaired with golden insights. And, you know, the truth. Or whatever.

2

Think Big, Move On

Boris Johnson has always thought big. Big Dog, big dreams. As a child he announced that he wanted to be 'world king'.[1] The role didn't technically exist then, and still doesn't, so you can imagine his disappointment when he found out. And then his flinty resolve. Yes, actually, he would be the *first* world king.

At the age of 12, he shrugged and officially downgraded his ambition to prime minister, which was as it turned out much more doable. It didn't end well, but perhaps it's merely unfinished business. 'Hasta la vista, baby!' he said in his valedictory speech to the House of Commons.[2] Who's to say he *won't* return in the future as the first world king? It would be *so Boris*.

Johnson zip-wired into politics from journalism because no one puts up statues to journalists.[3] That may have sounded selfish to some, but it wasn't. You usually only get a statue if you've done something important for your country; he was clearly focusing on his future service to the nation. Not all politicians get statues – our public spaces would look very crowded if they did – but then not all politicians have the nerve and the guts to go big. One thinks of Alexander the Great. Or Sargon of Akkad. Or Trump of Mar-a-Lago.

As mayor of London, Johnson embarked upon a series of grand civic projects. Of course he was let down, frustrated by a combination of small-mindedness, impossible engineering briefs, stupid financial miscalculations, inattention to detail, et cetera. None of which was his fault. He wasn't interested in 'process'. He was interested in vision, the bolder the better.

What he has in abundance is enthusiasm, and he can hose that out for minutes at a time. Turn him on to an idea he likes and he'll gush at full power, right up to the point where it clearly isn't going to work. Then, understandably, he'll turn off his hose, look around for something else, find it, then turn on his visionary gush for that instead. Sensible enthusiasm husbandry, a keynote of his life.

Be More Boris: The Big Lesson here is have a vision for your life. Have several. Have many. If one vision doesn't work out, have another. Don't be disheartened when the latest vision turns out to be wildly misguided, ill-thought-through, self-aggrandising or stupid. Simply refocus on the next.

Building a Bridge to the Future

The Garden Bridge project was an unhinged idea – as in, a closed door of 'little thinking' unhinged from its doorframe in order to create a bigger space, allowing 'big thinking' to flourish. Imagine: a bridge across the Thames, full not of horrible traffic but of *garden*! A grand project to stand as a monument to Mayor of London Boris Johnson's civic vision, far into the future.

And Boris knew how to get things done. Bish! He rugby-tackled the planning system. Bash! He informally decided upon the architects and engineers *before* a competition to choose the architects and engineers.[4] Bosh! He promised everyone it would be privately funded.

OK, it ended up costing taxpayers £43 million even though it was never built, but that wasn't his fault. Blame cruel fate. Investors proved elusive, the estimated cost rose from £60 million to £200 million, funding became more dependent on pumping up development potential either end of the bridge, there would be restrictions on public access, it would have to shut for corporate events or maybe even have an Apple store in the middle. It had spiralled away from viability, into liability.

Boris Johnson bravely refused to appear before the official inquiry into the failed project, declaring that he still fervently believed in it, before moving swiftly on to the next worthy recipient of his enthusiasm.

Be More Boris: If you believe in something, stick with it until the very end. Then swiftly walk away. Projects may come and go, but unbridled enthusiasm is forever.

The scale of your ambition is not important, it's your Borisivity that you're looking to unlock. Let's say you want to spend a couple of hundred quid on an indoor Grecianesque fountain with rotating colour palette and pulsing LED lights. Late one night, on the internet, you find a beauty.

Your partner's not keen. The money could be more usefully spent on groceries, or on one of several outstanding utility bills. But, you argue, where's the joy in that? Why, you say Borisly, this indoor folly would gladden our hearts every day. It would be a, er, er, VAJAZZLE on the *mons pubis* of our living room!

'It's fucking horrible,' says your partner. 'We're not getting it. Anyway, shut up, you sound like Boris Johnson.' 'Don't worry, leave all the paperwork to the wonga guys, they'll...' 'Sorry? What wonga guys? Why do we need wonga guys for a 200 quid monstrosity?' You confess to misreading the price. It actually costs £20,000, plus it now has to be installed. And the loan people wanted some wonga up front, so you took one of your mates out for lunch – the one who has his own IT business – and charmed a loan out of *him*... Your partner issues an ultimatum: it's me or the monstrosity.

Do what Boris would do. Tell your partner they're right: stupid impulse buy, you'll cancel it. But secretly you resolve to buy it anyway, then line up another chum to help pay back the first chum who lent you the money to pay the wonga guys. Chat up a possible new partner who might tolerate the monstrosity, ask them if they fancy shacking up together, then see if they'll lend you a bit of money to tide you over. If they do, go for an expensive lunch with someone else.

Don't Be an Island

A new airport in the Thames Estuary? Why not? It's just dead water bordered by a bleak, muddy wilderness. And everyone likes airports.

The scheme, very early on, acquired the tag 'Boris Island' which *sounds* like fun.[5] Adjacent vibe to Love Island – muddy but with a very obscure postcode for discreet liaisons. In 2013, when Johnson was London mayor, he enthusiastically talked up plans to build a six-runway airport, built entirely on an artificial island. The projected cost was around £47 billion, although by the time it was scrapped the estimate was over £100 billion, which sounds *much* more appropriate for a ~~world king~~ London mayor.[6] Boris Island cost £5 million of public money and still failed.[7] It all seemed like a colossal arse ache when you could just put another runway at Heathrow.

When he was elected as the MP for Uxbridge and South Ruislip in 2015, Johnson promised he would 'lie down in front of those bulldozers and stop the construction of that third runway'.[8] Three years later, when he was foreign secretary, there was a Commons vote on the third runway at Heathrow and Boris was faced with a horrible dilemma. Vote with the government in favour of the runway and betray his constituents or vote against it and resign his government position.

He took the only honourable option and managed to be in Afghanistan when the vote took place.[9] That way he didn't let his constituents down, he didn't let the government down, but most of all he didn't let himself down. Of course, his detractors hated it. This was Borisivity at its most discreet and valorous.

> **Be More Boris:** It's OK to let down people who are counting on you as long as that ends up being the best thing for everyone, which obviously includes you. It's important to move forward and move on.

You can take your own political shortcuts in life, like our hero, at any level. Let's say you've entered politics as the new chairwoman of your local parish council. Let's call you Caroline. As usual, this evening's meeting is dominated by a bad-tempered discussion about traffic. Commuters use the parish's back streets as a shortcut to the A11, turning once-quiet neighbourhoods into hell on wheels. Traffic calming hasn't worked – even with speed bumps, it's still a convenient rat-run.

You have a plan, and you've invited a local journalist along to hear it. Why doesn't the council build its *own* shortcut to the A11, entirely bypassing the quiet parish streets? Everyone agrees you've been at the fortified kombucha again, but you persist. If you could get a new road built, this would be the Parish Council That Actually Got Something Done.

Factoring in compensation, you estimate the 'Caroline Bypass' would cost in the region of £83 million. As to where it would go? That low-quality scrubland behind the parish church, say, plus maybe a few back gardens would probably accommodate it. On a point of order, the treasurer points out the parish council has only £2,752 at its disposal. You are undeterred. You guarantee it won't cost the council a penny, then wink at the local journalist. Caroline Bypass. Yeah, nice ring to it.

A month later you're back with a revised version of the Caroline Bypass. You tell the council (and a smattering of national journalists) that the revised budget is £170 million, that it's twice as impressive, and there has been substantial private sector interest. You indicate a pair of young men in all-black casual wear and full-face masks. One of them makes 'gunfingers' at you. Yes, a local consortium of entrepreneurs needs to invest a great deal of cash via a lease-loan arrangement. Yes, they'd like the Caroline Bypass to be a toll road and are looking for us to stash half a mil immediately – here Gunfingers holds up a rustling binbag – no questions asked. The councillors just need to electronically sign this contract, thanks. You call for Any Other Business, bang your gavel before anyone can say anything, take a swig of fortified kombucha and start singing 'Caroline Bypass' to the tune of 'Waterloo Sunset'.

A month later, the parish council minus you is meeting a legal aid solicitor at a magistrates' court. The few assets the parish council own have been seized by an administrator. You, meanwhile, have relocated to the Midlands, where

you're standing as a Tory candidate in a safe seat, the unpleasantness of the Caroline Bypass scheme collapse behind you.
You look forward very much to representing your new constituents and launching the Caroline Freeport.

Bringing Nations Together

In 2018, Foreign Secretary Boris Johnson addressed the
annual conference of Northern Ireland's Democratic
Unionist Party. He told them something that he'd been
briefed they'd like a lot. He said he was in favour of a
massive bridge between Scotland and Northern Ireland.

For years, engineers had fantasised about what would
be the longest structure of its kind in the world and how
it might be done. Well, here was a chance to find out!
Of course, the usual moaners hated the idea a lot more
once it had mysteriously acquired its nickname: the 'Boris
Bridge'. They derided it as yet another vanity project, of
course they did.

Excuses for abandoning it included a seabed trench
along the route filled with millions and millions of tonnes
of munitions, dumped there last century. Team Boris kept
impatiently shouting 'Well just blow the sodding lot up
now and get it over with. Or put, like, a very heavy blan-
ket over it all?' No luck, it was abandoned.

Any bridge between Scotland and Northern Ireland
would be the longest span bridge built to date. Any tunnel would be the longest undersea tunnel ever built. That
was the whole point, idiots! Boris Bridge, Boris Burrow.

One way or the other, the longest link in the world, with 'Boris' in the nickname! Ah well, at least Big Ideas Dog quickly forgot about it and moved on to something else, as all visionaries must.

> Be More Boris: If you can get people to believe in something stupidly big, you're not deluding them, you're giving them stupidly big hope. If you can imagine something impossible with your name attached, it's possible.

Let's say you're an average person living a reasonably normal life. Your partner comes down one morning to find you exercising in the kitchen. 'What's going on?' 'Oh,' you say, 'I'm just getting myself fit. You remember that time Boris Johnson invited the press to photograph him doing press-ups after he'd recovered from COVID, to show he was "as fit as a butcher's dog"? And then used it as a metaphor for how Britain could "bounce back" after the coronavirus lockdown by building infrastructure projects?' 'Yes,' says your partner bitterly. 'Well,' you say, 'that's what I'm doing. Getting fit enough to do something incredible. Something most people wouldn't even dream of trying.'

'How many press-ups did you manage?' asks your partner, introducing an unwelcome note of scepticism into the conversation. 'One,' you say, 'but I'll do more tomorrow, and the next day. I'm on a fast-track fitness route to the, er, er, sunlit uplands of endurance and achievement.

One thinks of Diagoras of Rhodes, who competed in the Olympic Games. How does that poem go...'

'Why have you suddenly gone all weird?' Your partner looks a little worried now. You announce to your partner, a little tetchily, that you plan to swim the Atlantic. There's a gratifying moment of awe as they take this in. But you can't even *swim*! 'All in good time,' you say. 'Press-ups, then swimming lessons, then practice, then the Atlantic Ocean.' Your partner urgently suggests you book in to see the GP. Swimming the Atlantic sounds like one of those mad GoFundMe things where gullible people chip in a fiver each for someone to do something impossible for charity and then it turns out there wasn't a charity at all, it was just a scam.

You consider this for a moment, hand your partner your phone and ask them to take a picture of you sort-of doing a press-up. Yes, maybe if your partner doesn't believe in you, there's a whole internet full of people who need to channel their hopes and dreams into a third-party champion of the absurd. Yes, you think. It'll be *Borissimo*.

And you'd be right. Reality is one thing, self-belief is another. Ignore everyone else who disagrees with you. Listen to yourself. That way, self-belief works 100 per cent of the time.

3

Transgress to Progress

The first lesson drawn from Boris Johnson's journalism – indeed, life – probably comes too late for anyone reading this, as it requires you to have had a private education, ideally with some desultory work experience on a university magazine. That, and his posh scallywag charm, got him a couple of introductions to the, er, er, thoroughly INTOXICATING world of journalism with its inspiring war cry: IMPLE SPATIUM. Or in the more rugged Anglo-Saxon rendering: FILL THE FUCKING SPACE.

Johnson entered the world of national journalism in 1988 at *The Times* HQ, where he was given a slot down-desk in the newsroom, mostly doing rewrites of PR handouts. The skill any young journalist quickly learns is to make a story more interesting. Boris overstepped the mark and (worse) was found out, then sacked. He fabricated a quote in an otherwise quite boring piece he wrote about the possible discovery of the remains of a palace built by Edward II.[1]

He had telephoned his godfather, Dr Colin Lucas, for some historical background and then boosted the story by quoting him saying the palace was where the king kept Piers Gaveston, his 'catamite' (what ordinary newspaper readers might call a teenage sex slave). Unfortunately, poor Piers was executed years before the palace was even built. Of course, Lucas complained, so Johnson did the only sensible thing given the circumstances – he doubled down by writing a follow-up story saying that the mystery had deepened around the date of the castle. It got complicated, he was fired, but at least he stuck to his guns.

A teachable moment. Sometimes the only honourable thing to do is to defend the integrity of the lie by repeating it. Years later Boris acknowledged that 'of all the mistakes I made, I think that takes the biscuit.'

Be More Boris: If you have knowingly done something bad, call it a mistake. Everybody makes those. If you regret your actions, that's the first step in the healing process. Self-forgiveness is easy: you made a simple 'mistake'. Or, if you prefer, 'biscuit'.

Don't Apologise – Forgive Yourself, Edit Yourself

What journalism also taught Our Intrepid Reporter is the power of editing. All of us have incidents we'd rather erase from our memory. Scoop Dog's no exception. It serves no useful purpose to remember that in 1990 Boris Johnson agreed to give an acquaintance the address of a reporter whom the acquaintance wanted beaten up.[2] Johnson doesn't need to remember it – he later dismissed the whole thing as a joke – so neither do we. We can edit our memories. There's absolutely no point in beating ourselves up about these things, or indeed anyone else.

Think of your life as a news story. It's still unfolding, of course, but at any given moment you can publish an update – a sort of Life Bulletin. Even better, you can edit your story to remove any accusation of blame. Whatever you did, you have nothing to apologise for. It was an error in the story, it's been corrected now, an apology is pointless. Yes, this is the news today, but nobody will be reading it tomorrow…

If you're considering offering an apology for something 'they' say you've done, STOP. It's perfectly possible to apologise without apologising for everyday misdemeanours, from forgetting to empty the dishwasher to first-degree murder. 'I hold my hands up' we say, giving ourselves the respect we deserve. Then, just as someone might reasonably be expecting you to say, 'I'm sorry. I don't know what happened. That's exactly the sort of thing I'd never do…', maybe give a little shrug.

You've learned from this incident. You've grown as a person. An apology helps nobody, least of all you.

Be More Boris: You're a work in progress. You can't change Future You, and Present You is obviously perfect, but you can always edit Past You. Because if you 'did' something, it's in the past. And the past is written by the victor – in this case, obviously you.

Here are some examples of how to edit past wrong-doing into future self-forgiveness:

'Yes, I embezzled six hundred grand from the company. I have had a word with myself and I'm now ready to draw a line under it.'

'Yes, I deliberately poisoned next door's dog. I'm not particularly proud of what I did, and I accept that errors of judgement occurred, chiefly the poisoning. Now I feel as though I'm ready to move on without rancour or recrimination, and I invite you to do the same.'

'Yes, I drove a car after sinking eight pints and three Jägerbombs, came off the road and ploughed into a food bank. Obviously, there are regrets, but I'm pleased to report that I have come to terms with the wrong turning, both in life and the road, I inadvertently took.'

'Yes, I set fire to my local library because I'd been told – erroneously, as I later found out – that it was the location of a paedophile ring. I regret my course of action and the destruction of what I now know to be simply a library. But let's remember I was told about the paedo thing by other people, so the original guilt ultimately is theirs. Thankfully, I have found it in my heart to forgive myself, I cannot speak for others.'

'Yes, I understand that certain people believe I lied to the House of Commons and the Queen, but even if I were to acknowledge those alleged misbehaviours as two separate mistakes sort of squashed together to make a bigger one, it probably wouldn't be as bad as that making up a quote thing.'

You Can Smash This – Just Be Funny

Even the harshest critics of Boris Johnson concede, through gritted teeth, that he was and remains a great journalistic entertainer. He has a deep understanding of the craft – how to capture an audience, how to keep them entranced.

Johnson was Brussels correspondent for the *Telegraph*, at a time when Thatcherism was roaring through its Loadsamoney period, and the EU was roundly mocked by the right-wing press as a bureaucratic monster coming after the freedoms of ordinary people.[3] And nobody, it turned out, could be quite as monstering, quite as daft, about the EU as Scoop Dog. Reminiscing in 2005 on *Desert Island Discs* he said 'I was sort of chucking these rocks over the garden wall and I listened to this amazing crash from the greenhouse next door over in England as everything I wrote from Brussels was having this amazing, explosive effect on the Tory party. And it really gave me this, I suppose, rather weird sense of power…'[4]

In 1991, under the headline 'Italy fails to measure up on condoms',[5] Johnson wrote: 'Brussels bureaucrats have shown their legendary attention to detail by rejecting new specifications for condom dimensions'. He said that Italian men required smaller condoms. Italian men then angrily asserted their dick size was normal. An EU spokesman, Willy Hélin, was quoted as saying that it was 'a very serious business.' Fast-forward to 2019, and a retired Hélin told the *Guardian* it had 'nothing to do with the size of dicks'. It was about assessing sexual risks for AIDS patients. Talk about undermining a future British prime minister. 'He was a clown – a successful clown...' Yes, exactly, matey: *successful*.

Be More Boris: You CAN make it up. A lie isn't a lie if it's a joke. Your self-assurance in standing by the joke is what makes it in the end a form of higher truth about human existence – enjoy!

Your partner comes home from work exhausted, the ingredients for dinner abandoned by the cooker. They see you sitting bolt upright in a chair, holding a slip of paper and a pencil, looking glazed and immobile.

'Oh, God,' they sigh. 'If you've been banging tequila again instead of cooking our dinner... Honestly, I will... What the hell is wrong?' You don't make eye contact. You *can't* make eye contact. You have to look at the slip. It looks like a supermarket till receipt. 'Sit down', you say quietly. 'Sit down and read me the numbers on that piece of paper.' Now they're intrigued. They read out the numbers.

You show them the slip you're holding. It's a ticket for Wednesday's lottery draw. Today's Wednesday. They've just announced the numbers. They are the same numbers. You show them your phone. Wednesday's lottery draw. The numbers are the same. You appear to be struggling to breathe as you tell your partner the prize for six correct numbers is Three. Million. Pounds. Sterling.

A moment of silence, like in *Oppenheimer* just before the bomb's rush of noise. 'I don't believe this,' they say, scrambling to find the tequila. Three million pounds. Oh, my giddy FUCK! They throw their arms around you, unable even to grasp the size or shape of this enormous, hilarious mushroom cloud of happy-lucky... WAIT.

You're smirking. You show them the date on the slip. This Wednesday. You indicate the numbers on the screen. LAST Wednesday. You simply bought a ticket using the same numbers for this Wednesday's draw, then pulled up the online page for last week's result as well.

For several seconds they echo your earlier glazed immobility. They then gather their things, wordlessly head for the door, think again, return to give you a big slap, then swish out, slamming the door.

Deep inside, you KNOW that one day they'll look back on this evening. You may no longer be a couple, but they will remember it for ever. And it will be funny. It definitely will be. And they'll maybe be laughing AT you, but they'll also be laughing with you. Yes, you lied, but it was a bloody good joke, eh? Honk honk!

Resilience Is a Superpower

Even those killjoys exasperated by Scoop Dog's journalistic liberties acknowledged his ability to successfully satirise politics. He'd found his niche. He'd built a garden bridge, if you will, between journalism and politics. He could do both brilliantly, and to both he would return.

Behind the vivid journalism was a buffoonish character. And underneath the buffoonery was an extremely likeable

bloke hungry for fame, fortune and power. And underneath THAT was a genuinely brilliant guy who lives his
life according to the Chumbawamba Principle: *Si percus-
sus fuero, resurrecturus sum.*

He left politics, he came back. He left journalism, he
came back. Hasta la vista, Boris the Returninator. These
days, in what we must all hope is a breather between political careers, he's back doing greenhouse-smashing social
commentary in his column for the *Mail on Sunday*. It's,
er, er, Maximum Bojo, the world fractured by the kalei-
doscopic, hyperbolic, expialidocious, er, er, what-not
of a fundamentally kind and clever man railing against
whatever occurs in his GALACTIC brain two hours
before copy deadline. Politics, culture wars, bicycles, who
knows? He's like a great lumbering William McGonagall
poem in human form.

But. Could he... be prime minister again? From his
lofty new position as 'self-exonerated, former prime minister and informal political consultant', he now freely
offers advice to the Conservative party. 'When we get
back in,' he wrote in July 2024, 'don't be too hasty to get
rid of successful election-winning leaders... As I never
tire of telling people, some polls put us only two or three
points behind in the days before I was forced to resign in
what was really a media-driven hoo-ha.'[6]

Resilience. Johnson just keeps at it. He's not counting
anything out. And there's a pleasing closing of the circle
here. Where once the young Boris would *inflate* a non-
story into a media-driven hoo-ha, now old Boris *deflates*

an actual story about him by dismissing it as just that. He is, let's face it, brilliant. And with any luck, unstoppable.

> Be More Boris: Never give up. Whatever it was, it was just a media-driven hoo-ha. Retreat, reset, return. If the audience doesn't get you, change the audience.

You've moved to a new area. The neighbours are friendly. You've been invited to join the local WhatsApp group, which is, you discover, a really useful and support-ive forum of helpful people. In the first week, you get rec-ommendations for a roofer and a plumber. It's all a bit dull though, after a while. Oh look, someone's lost a cat. You notice that they get loads of sympathy. Much more than you got when you complained about a cat shitting in your garden.

Clearly this is an emotional readership. What might it take for you to have an impact? You delete the unloved post about the shitting cat and try to make amends by inventing three cats of your own who have all gone miss-ing overnight. There's some sympathy sure, but also a little scepticism. You decide to gamble everything by put-ting the wind up everybody.

'Just thought I'd flag that when I spoke to the police yes-terday about the sudden disappearance of Calyx, Tiberius and Umbra, I heard some rather unwelcome news. I don't wish to alarm my fellow cat-parents, but it seems as though this has been happening sporadically all over town for a month or so. Extremely sinister... Meanwhile, if anyone

spots any of my three (pics below) I would be most grateful for any information. I would pay a handsome reward
to get them back.'

As you thought, the group explodes into speculation
about the terrible fate of the cats. You're persuaded to
share what little information you have, which is that the
disappearances always happen at night. You tap into a
familiar combination of paranoia and compulsion to 'do
something' and suggest that, as usual, neither the police
nor the council can keep our cats safe, and that it may
be time to turn vigilante. You suggest a Cat Patrol – no
firearms but bats with nails through acceptable – to try
and catch the pussy-grabbers and deliver them to justice.
You're a hero.

Oh, one of the WhatsAppers knows a senior copper
at the local nick who has grave reservations about your
story and would like to meet you all to get to the bot-
tom of the rumours. Bing-bong! A small delegation of
neighbours is at your door. You're as shocked as they
are. Perhaps the person you spoke to originally was
impersonating a police officer? 'Impersonating them? At
the police station?' asks one busybody, theatrically. It's
a fair cop. You confess the whole thing was an inverted
pyramid of piffle. You made it up. Not for yourself, but
for the common good. To instil vigilance and, er, er,
UNITY and, er, er… Everyone's more disappointed
than cross, which is worse.

You stay off the WhatsApp chat for a month or so, but
the temptation is too much. 'I hope we've all been able to

put that last media hoo-ha behind us now. Just wanted to alert everyone to a gross overreach by the council who, I have it on good authority, are poised to declare cars illegal, if you can believe it!' You're permanently removed from the group.

Just the wrong audience, that's all. You find a real curtain-twitching, stranger-danger online set-up called Off My Lawn. You float the cat thing; other people claim to have heard the same rumour and are clearly fabricating their own pets to have them go missing too. You're a hero again. You mention the 'illegal cars' rumour. Someone says it's already started in Bradford, under Sharia law. Finally, your persistence has paid off. Your audience is lapping it up. All that nasty stuff people said about the lying. You can ignore them now. You have the correct audience. Resilience wins, again.

4

Be Yourself, Repeat Yourself

A lot of self-improvement books are just that: ways of re-inventing yourself, making yourself a 'better person'. Changing who you are. But what the Life of Boris tells us is that, as long as you're happy with who you are, there's no NEED to change. At all. Just keep being you on repeat – that way, more people get to see the perfected version.

His enemies accuse Sensei Boris of having no character, which is just an old-fashioned way of claiming he adheres to no moral code whatsoever. They should perhaps join the rest of us in the twenty-first century. There have been huge changes in the way we – and especially the media – appraise people these days. You don't need character if you have a personality. And you don't even need a personality if you have a persona.

The version of Boris we all love – the, er, er, UNHINGED, ruffled Old English Sheepdog with his mop hair and his marvellous HEADSTRONG lunge through life, his, er, er, *vive ut vivas*, his self-deprecating demeanour – arrived in prototype at Oxford Union debates. He was good at arguing, clever and funny. He was a dazzling charmer then, and he's been a successfully dazzling charmer ever since. Perfect.

> Be More Boris: Find a persona that suits you; be that persona on repeat. Resist all temptation to improve or rehinge yourself, you're perfect.

Keep your Love Life Interesting

Of course, judgemental bores everywhere may disapprove of any relationship that has its ups and downs, its minor transgressions, but surely this is just *another* reason to adore mercurial Boris the Lover – as if we needed one! Being in a relationship with him must be like travelling downhill in a romantic runaway bus with no brakes or suspension, or like being on some crazy sex-rollercoaster. Exciting! 'The course of true love never did run smooth', as Shakespeare wrote in *A Midsummer Night's Dream*.

Yes, OK, Shakespeare didn't have Hermia tell Lysander that he'd fucked up her white sofa with red wine and that 'You just don't care for anything because you're spoilt!' And he didn't have Lysander shout 'Get off my fucking laptop!' How very typical of the Boris-undermining *Guardian* to have run this story, claiming it was a transcript of a recording made by a concerned neighbour, one month before Johnson became prime minister.[1]

Of course, it made no difference. Why should it? If there's one thing connecting all the stories of wronged women throughout the love life of our Casanova of Westminster, it's a weary nation adjusting its bosom, taking a long drag on a Marlboro Light, squinting into the distance and sighing 'You must have known what he was like, love.'

Nobody's saying he's a *type*, but there is a pattern, and it basically goes Snog, Marry, Avoid, with 'snog' as euphemism. Until now, he's been that poor, hapless guy at the centre of every Brian Rix farce, minus his trousers in the wardrobe. He gets married, adultery occurs as if by osmosis, she has enough, the other woman becomes the primary woman, and on and on it goes. So, whose fault is that? Not his. We'll find out why shortly – it's a medical thing – but meanwhile here's the life lesson…

Be More Boris: If romantic partners cannot tolerate you when you're repeatedly cheating, they don't deserve you when you're repeatedly faithful.

You and your flatmate have set off for a lovely day in the countryside. Eventually. The car packed, she couldn't find you anywhere, so rang your mobile. 'What do you mean you're down at the canal feeding the ducks? I thought we were going to set off first thing.' 'God, all right. Calm down, there's no rush. It's bloody Sunday.'

Eventually you return to the flat, where she seems very cross and impatient. 'How has it taken you a bloody hour to get back here?' Two can play at that game. You snap back that the countryside's not going anywhere, is it? It's not going to get all used up by the time we get there, is it?

Twenty minutes into your walk, she turns round to find you gone. How? You were like ten yards behind her a minute ago. You, meanwhile, have found a shortcut to the very village pub where you'd both planned to reach by a circuitous route in about two hours. Oh, and they're just opening for lunch, too. Your phone goes, it's her. You dismiss the call, switch off your phone. That's what you're supposed to do isn't it – live in the moment. Ooh, look! A fancy steak and ale pie on the specials board. You put your phone away and find the map you'd both brought so you didn't get lost. Not to worry, you think. She can use Google Maps if there's a signal.

Three hours later you're rudely woken up by a car door slamming. It's your flatmate in tears. She got very lost, eventually came across some hikers who were heading in the right direction and has now turned up to find you sleeping off a pub lunch. It's fuming no-speaks all the way home, then time for the inevitable row. Throughout, you remain commendably calm. She's ranting about being deserted, abandoned without warning, when it was supposed to be a lovely day out together.

You turn your back on her to look coolly out of the window. You point out that you at least have had a lovely day, and that the pie was top class. And you tell her to get some perspective. You live in the same flat, so technically over the last, say, 24 hours you've either been within earshot or both been asleep under the same roof for an overwhelming majority of that time. You think she's being entirely unreasonable, she's not your boss, and you think it's time you both looked for new flatmates. You turn around, but she's left the room. Ah well, *c'est la vie*.

You Can't Change the Way You Are

Andrew Gimson, in *Boris Johnson: The Rise and Fall of a Troublemaker at Number 10*, tells us how the painter Celia Montague discovered his 'two charming physical characteristics… a lovely warm chest voice with a great bubble of laughter and enjoyment in it [and] a quirk of the mouth that makes him look both shy and mischievous at the same time.'[2]

I mean, you can absolutely hear him, can't you? And that look. It's him, isn't it? The Boris who ruffled and shuffled his way into a nation's heart. The loveable clown. The smooth cad. It's not an easy look to pull off, that intoxicating mix of Terry-Thomas and Mr Blobby, but he manages it superbly, and we love him for it. Anyway, 'pull off' suggests he's trying, putting on an act, as his critics ceaselessly allege.

But Boris Johnson is not pulling off anything. 'I haven't had to have a wank for 20 years,' he once boasted, although that was a while ago.[3] Maybe he's had one recently, but it really is none of our business, is it? None of our business at all. Quite a lot has been made of his prodigal sexuality. So what? He can't help it. Let's not be too prurient, but it sounds like some sort of medical condition.

Sonia Purnell, his deputy in the *Telegraph*'s Brussels office in the early 1990s, says he once explained to another man that, though married, he needed affairs because 'he was literally busting with spunk'.[4] It's a horrible, terrifying thought and he surely deserves our sympathy.

Someone so compellingly attractive, so sexually available, is bound to inspire serial attention – none of this is his fault. This bears repeating, not least by him. *Not his fault*. He is as God made him. It's as God also made John F. Kennedy, let's remember. JFK was a philanderer but also a great statesman, and today is recognised merely by his initials. ABdPJ, as history will surely one day fondly remember him is, like Kennedy, a national and global treasure. His political achievements entirely eclipse his sexual peccadillos. Leave him alone, he's explained that he's a pressure cooker full of semen and needs to let off 'steamen' every so often.

But perhaps that's all in the past now he's settled down, had another couple of children and is devoted to his wife. That might even explain why he's apparently put on so much weight lately: spunk backlog. For goodness sake, keep him away from anything erotic. He'll go off like a water cannon!

Be More Boris: Explain to your partner that whatever it is they don't like about you is an incurable condition and that you have a doctor's note and a repeat prescription for it.

Starting a relationship with someone new can be tricky if you have a 'reputation'. But building a life together requires a lot of planning, a lot of preparation. If you can see the obstacles ahead, you can avoid them by having your excuses ready in advance.

You cannot be 'overprepared'. As the relationship develops, it's possible your partner might pick up on one or two of your less appealing characteristics. It's well worth your anticipating this. On the face of it, having actual doctor's notes, or statements from psychiatrists, or the discreetly qualified testimonials of sexual health consultants may seem crass, but you can make them look smarter by having them laminated and framed with an official-looking black border.

Some suggestions, and remember: it doesn't matter that they're fake if what they're saying is true.

'I declare that the cardholder is an accredited patient in need of emergency sex and a bloody decent person as well. If you have been handed this card, please, if you can, offer any remedial sexual assistance you feel able to provide. Signed, Dr. Harold Shipman, M.D.'

'The bearer of this laminated card is entitled to a minimum of THREE bunga-bunga parties in a Bavarian castle courtesy of me, the undersigned, His Royal Highness Colin Dracula, Emperor of Honkvania.'

'As chair of H.M. Government's Interdepartmental Panel of Approved Liberties, I hereby allow the cardholder to behave in accordance with all declared desires, incurring no moral judgements or ethical prohibitions whatsoever, in the name of God. Signed, Billy Banter Esq, Parliament, London.'

Formula You – Worth Repeating

The broadcaster Jeremy Vine remembers some years back being on the same bill as The Greatest Political Entertainer of his Generation, when Boris Johnson was a backbench Tory MP. It was an awards ceremony at a swish hotel, where Vine was to hand out awards for 'International Securitisation', and Johnson was to give the after-dinner speech. At 9.28pm, with two minutes to go: 'BOOM! A rush of wind from an opened door, a golden mop, a heave of body and dinner jacket onto the chair next to mine, and the breathless question: "JEREMY. Where exactly AM I?" '⁵

He was late, clearly hadn't prepared a speech, and was due onstage in ninety seconds. Vine himself felt he was in some terrible stress dream. The late arrival asked someone nearby to explain securitisation, then asked urgently for a pen and paper. Vine noticed at the top of the page he'd scribbled 'SHEEP' and 'SHARK' before Boris was announced and ushered to the stage.

Now, suddenly, it looks as if a catastrophe is about to unfold. Then, to find out where he is, he turns slowly around and reads the large on-screen logo aloud, triumphantly. The crowd cheers, loving this chaotic star turn. He tells a rambling story about his uncle's farm and how EU regulations mean he has to ring someone at an abattoir

50 miles away. 'His name was Mick... No, it was Jim...
No, sorry, MARGARET. That was it, MARGARET...'
People are soon roaring with laughter. He continues with
a bit about why his political hero is the town mayor from
JAWS because he kept the beach open, even if it meant a
couple of small children being eaten. Then a famous story
about politician George Brown, *but he forgets the punchline*. The evening's a huge success. Everyone loves him.

Eighteen months later, Vine is at another awards ceremony. The speaker is Boris Johnson. He arrives as before,
minutes before he's due to go on and has again to be
reminded of the occasion, again asks for a pen and paper,
again scribbles notes and – BANG! – he's on stage. He
appears to have forgotten where he is. He turns to shyly
read the event off the screen. Then, as before, the story
about the abattoir: 'Mick... No, Jim... No, MARGARET.'
Then the mayor from *JAWS* routine, with exactly the
same details, then the story with the forgotten punchline.
Vine cannot believe what he's watching. 'Now I understand everything. I realised that those two Boris speeches
had made me pose the fundamental question, the one that
concerns you most when you listen to a politician: Is this
guy for real?'[6]

What Boris Johnson understands is that everyone needs
happiness and reassurance in their lives. Was it not Horace
who REMINDED us that, er, er, how does it go, *dulce est
desipere in loco*, yes. It is sweet now and then to play the fool,
to – how would the great man have expressed it today? –
perhaps 'dick about and CHILL, man, honk honk!'

This story, by the way, originally appeared on Jeremy Vine's Facebook page. Then it was repeated *word for word* in *The Spectator*. Who's the hypocrite now, Mr Vine? The defence case rests, m'lud.

Be More Boris: If you're bringing happiness to people, how can it be wrong to do the same thing over and over again, therefore multiplying happiness? Repetition makes perfect!

As long as we have our routine worked out, there's no reason why any of us can't shine, repeatedly, in public. Let's say you've rehearsed your public persona. You're completely adorable, clearly very clever but with your sharp wisdom shrouded in a self-deprecating cloak of affability. Perhaps you're weirdly childish for someone that old, but it somehow just makes you more lovable.

Let's say you walk into a supermarket and take a carton of half a dozen eggs to the cashier. 'Hiya, alright? That'll be one pound eighty-five.' 'Oh, crikey. Oh, gawd,' you bluster. 'That can't be right, surely. They're not, er, er, Fabergé you know. Badoom-tish! Honk honk!' 'That's the price on them right there, sorry. They're free range. We have got non-free range?' 'No, it's all right,' you say. 'I'll take these. Tell you what, I'll give you one pound fifty. How's that?' 'Sorry, what?' 'One-point-five pounds sterling. Best and final offer.' 'But no, sorry, they're one-eighty-five…'

Here's your repeatable moment. You turn to the increasingly irritated queue behind you and bellow: 'I put it to this people's forum that it is precisely this intransigence, this inflexibility, that has seen Britain reduced from a once-mighty market-driven empire to a nation of, of, of – EGGS! Is this the socialist dream the Labour party has in store for us? All of us identical, *prix fixe*, reduced in effect to so much yolk and, er, er, ALBUMEN?'

People in the queue ask you to shut up or push off, or both, or ask if you're off your meds or something. Security has been summoned to Aisle Number 4. You sweep off, majestically. 'I am not an egg. I am a free man! *Ave atque vale!* Hail and farewell, until we meet again!'

You're obviously not going to meet that audience again, ever. You'll be lucky if you ever manage to get served there again. Congratulations. It may seem overwhelming now, but this is your future – roaming the land, haggling over the price of eggs and deploring the prospect of a Nation of Albumen, et cetera. It is merely a matter of time before showbusiness or politics or popular journalism discovers you and propels you to a More Boris You, a More YOU You. And honestly, everyone wishes you all the best.

Epilogue

In conclusion, the truth we have gleaned from the Life of Johnson is even more simple than 'believe in yourself'. The greatest life lesson Boris has taught us is this: BELIEVE YOURSELF.

What Boris shows us is the power of *re-truthing*. However at odds your truth is with everyone else's, yours is the only truth that matters. As long as you believe it, or at the very least pretend to believe it, you're golden. It's not your problem if nobody knows whether what you're saying is true or false. In fact, it makes you more interesting, clever and funny. Be More Boris and you too can be a riddle wrapped in a mystery hiding inside a fridge.[1]

Throughout his life, Boris has been a narrative genius. At prep school, he told his classmates he had a pet elephant at home called Fuckjumbo. He won a cross-country race at Eton by completing the middle section in a cab. He ended a relationship at Oxford University by taking the woman on a picnic and playing Elton John's 'Sorry Seems To Be The Hardest Word' quite badly on the recorder every time she asked him a question, then packed everything back into the BMW and just left her there. As mayor of London, he tried unsuccessfully to have the fourth plinth in Trafalgar Square occupied by a hologram of himself welcoming tourists to the heart of the city in 28 different languages. He has nicknamed his penis 'Mr President'.

The 'truth' is that everything in that last paragraph was false. The *truth*, however, is whatever you want it to be. 'We cannot turn our backs on Europe. We are part of Europe.'[2] Did he really once say that? Yes. Did he really once call George W. Bush 'a cross-eyed Texan warmonger, unelected, inarticulate, who epitomises the arrogance of American foreign policy.'[3] Yes. Did he really once describe the British electorate as 'the most fickle, feckless, capricious mob of wilfully ignorant mouth-breathing morons on the face of the fucking Earth…' No, obviously not. Or did he? No. Or 'did' he? 'No'.

What Boris shows us is that it's fine to reconstruct reality in a style of your choosing. Because, in the end, honesty is in the eye of the believer. In today's complex, fractured world, where real may be fake and intelligence may be artificial, the only truth we can trust is the one we construct for ourselves and for others. We should *all* be more ourselves. We should *all* Be More Boris.

NOTES

CHAPTER ONE: IF IT AIN'T FIXED, BREAK IT

1   'work round the clock' – Boris Johnson, PM statement in
    Downing Street: 13 December 2019 (https://www.gov.uk/
    government/speeches/pm-statement-in-downing-street-13-
    december-2019)

2   'only if all the Downing Street special advisers reported
    directly to him' – Richard Johnstone, 'Call for inquiry into
    Dominic Cumming's centralisation of special advisers', Civil
    Service World, 25th June 2020 (https://www.civilservicewo
    rld.com/professions/article/call-for-inquiry-into-dominic-
    cummingss-centralisation-of-special-advisers)

3   'deaths of over 230,000 British citizens have been related to
    COVID' – Michael Holden, 'British public were failed by
    flawed planning for COVID pandemic, inquiry finds', Reuters,
    19th July 2024 – (https://www.reuters.com/world/uk/
    uk-covid-inquiry-issue-first-report-preparedness-2024-07-17)

4   'solitary Queen at her husband's funeral' – David Mercer,
    'Prince Philip's funeral: Queen sits alone as she bids
    farewell to the Duke of Edinburgh', Sky News, 17th April
    2021 (https://news.sky.com/story/prince-philip-fune
    ral-queen-arrives-at-st-georges-chapel-ahead-of-minutes-sile
    nce-as-duke-of-edinburgh-is-laid-to-rest-12278005)

5   'wheeled clanking into the nation's HQ in a Samsonite travel
    case' – Chloe Chaplain and Jane Merrick, 'Staff used suitcase
    to ferry booze quietly into Downing Street', inews.co.uk, 14th
    January 2022

6   'the 40 new hospitals' – 'Building work pending for many of
40 promised hospitals', BBC News, 17th May 2023 (https://
www.bbc.co.uk/news/health-65607962)

CHAPTER TWO: THINK BIG, MOVE ON
1   'world king' – 'Boris Johnson: The boy who wanted to be
world king', BBC Newsnight (https://www.bbc.co.uk/
news/av/uk-politics-49088773)
2   'Hasta la vista, baby' – Sophie Morris, 'Terminated Boris
Johnson signs off with 'Hasta la vista, baby' in final PMQs,
Sky News, 20th July 2020 (https://news.sky.com/story/ter
minated-boris-johnson-signs-off-with-hasta-la-vista-baby-in-f
inal-pmqs-12655569)
3   'no one puts up statues to journalists' – Andrew Rawnsley,
'Boris Johnson clings to office like chewing gum to a
shoe but he is becoming unstuck', the *Observer*, 24th
April 2022 (https://www.theguardian.com/commentisf
ree/2022/apr/24/boris-johnson-clings-to-office-like-chew
ing-gum-on-shoe-becoming-unstuck)
4   'He informally decided upon the architects and engineers
before a competition' – Rupert Neate and Esther Addley, 'You
pay for it, chum': Johnson's struggle to save his garden bridge,
the *Guardian*, 16th July 2019 (https://www.theguardian.
com/politics/2019/jul/16/you-pay-for-it-chum-boris-john
son-struggle-save-garden-bridge)
5   'Boris Island' – Gwyn Topham, 'Boris Island' airport: how,
what where?, the *Guardian*, 18th January 2012 (https://www.
theguardian.com/politics/2012/jan/18/boris-island-airp
ort-what-where)
6   'by the time it was scrapped' – Billy Kenber, 'Boris Island
airport plan is rejected as too costly at £100bn', *The Times*,
2nd September 2014 (https://www.thetimes.com/article/
boris-island-airport-plan-is-rejected-as-too-costly-at-100bn-
8gkv76f82pl)

7   'Boris Island cost £5 million of public money and still failed' –
    Robin de Peyer, 'Boris Johnson defends £5m cost of failed
    Thames Estuary Airport scheme', the *Standard*, 3rd October
    2014 (https://www.standard.co.uk/news/london/boris-john
    son-defends-ps5m-cost-of-failed-thames-estuary-airport-sch
    eme-9770249)

8   'lie down in front of those bulldozers' – Damian Carrington,
    'Heathrow third runway ruled illegal over climate change',
    the *Guardian*, 27th February 2020 (https://www.theguard
    ian.com/environment/2020/feb/27/heathrow-third-run
    way-ruled-illegal-over-climate-change)

9   'managed to be in Afghanistan when the vote took place' –
    Heather Stewart, 'Boris Johnson trip on day of Heathrow
    vote cost taxpayer £20,000', the *Guardian*, 15th August 2018
    (https://www.theguardian.com/politics/2018/aug/15/
    controversial-trip-by-boris-johnson-on-day-of-key-vote-cos
    t-20000#:~:text=The%20government%20comfortably%20
    won%20the,his%20promise%20to%20his%20constituents)

CHAPTER THREE: TRANSGRESS TO PROGRESS

1   'He fabricated a quote' – Clare Dwyer Hogg, 'My greatest
    mistake. Boris Johnson, MP for Henley and editor of *The
    Spectator*, the *Independent*, 21st May 2002 (https://www.inde
    pendent.co.uk/news/media/my-greatest-mistake-boris-john
    son-mp-for-henley-and-editor-of-the-spectator-189322)

2   'a reporter whom the acquaintance wanted beaten up' – Simon
    Murphy, 'Reporter who Boris Johnson conspired to have
    beaten up demands apology, the *Guardian*, 14th July 2019
    (https://www.theguardian.com/politics/2019/jul/14/jou
    rnalist-stuart-collier-boris-johnson-phone-call-darius-guppy-
    demands-apology)

3   'a bureaucratic monster coming after the freedoms of ordinary
    people – Jon Henley, 'Is the EU really dictating the shape of
    your bananas?', the *Guardian*, 11th May 2016 (https://www.

theguardian.com/politics/2016/may/11/boris-johnson-launches-the-vote-leave-battlebus-in-cornwall)

4   'Reminiscing in 2005 on Desert Island Discs' – Boris Johnson, Desert Island Discs, BBC Radio 4 (https://www.bbc.co.uk/programmes/p00935b6)

5   'Italy fails to measure up on condoms' – Jennifer Rankin and Jim Waterson, 'How Boris Johnson's Brussels-bashing stories shaped British politics', the *Guardian*, 14th July 2019.

6   'I was forced to resign in what was really a media-driven hoo-ha' – Boris Johnson, 'Starmer's majority is built on sand. It's a mile wide and an inch deep. Here's my ten-point guide to bashing Labour and getting back into power', *Daily Mail*, 5th July 2024 (https://www.dailymail.co.uk/debate/article-13604919/BORIS-JOHNSON-Starmers-majority-built-san d-mile-wide-inch-deep-ten-point-guide-bashing-Labour-gett ing-power)

CHAPTER FOUR: BE YOURSELF, REPEAT YOURSELF

1   'a transcript of a recording made by a concerned neighbour' – Jim Waterson, 'Boris Johnson: police called to loud altercation at potential PM's home', the *Guardian*, 21st June 2019 (https://www.theguardian.com/politics/2019/jun/21/pol ice-called-to-loud-altercation-at-boris-johnsons-home)

2   'two charming physical characteristics' – Andrew Gimson, *Boris Johnson: The Rise and Fall of a Troublemaker at Number 10*, Simon & Schuster, 2023 (paperback), page 155.

3   'I haven't had to have a wank for 20 years' – Stephen Robinson, 'Is Boris on an upward spiral at last?', *The Sunday Times*, 28th December 2008 (https://www.thetimes.com/arti cle/is-boris-on-an-upward-spiral-at-last-2zj5rfkq8ml)

4   'he was literally busting. with spunk' – Sonia Purnell, *Just Boris: A Tale of Blond Ambition*, Aurum, 2012 (paperback), page 270.

5 'Jeremy Vine remembers some years back being on the same bill' – Jeremy Vine, 'My Boris Johnson Story', *The Spectator*, 17th June 2019 (https://www.spectator.co.uk/article/my-boris-johnson-story/)

6 'Is this guy for real?' – Ibid.

EPILOGUE

1 'a mystery hiding inside a fridge' – Heather Stewart and Aamna Mohdin, 'Boris Johnson hides in a fridge' to avoid Piers Morgan interview, the *Guardian*, 11th December 2019 (https://www.theguardian.com/politics/2019/dec/11/boris-johnson-hides-in-fridge-to-avoid-piers-morgan-interview)

2 'We cannot turn our backs on Europe' – Jess Staufenberg, 'Boris Johnson Brexit speech: MP speaks out after Britain decides to leave EU', the *Independent*, 24th June 2016 (https://www.independent.co.uk/news/uk/politics/brexit-boris-johnson-speech-in-full-eu-referendum-who-will-be-next-prime-minister-uk-a7100566)

3 'a cross-eyed Texan warmonger' – David A. Graham, 'A short history of Boris Johnson insulting foreign leaders', the *Atlantic* (https://www.theatlantic.com/international/archive/2016/07/boris-johnsons-foreign-strained-relations/491237/)

ACKNOWLEDGEMENTS

Thanks to Eileen Martin for her help in researching this subject and her admirable lack of squeamishness. Thanks to everyone who's ever written about Johnson — I've almost certainly read it, or skimmed it, or at least bought it secondhand from Abe Books, even if specific credits didn't make the final cut. Thanks to my agents Abby and CJ from Casarotto Ramsay & Associates and Grace Paul from Bloomsbury, and to the magic of serendipity. Thanks to editor Rose Brown and to copy editor Lisa Pendreigh, who did such a brilliant job and made some really clever suggestions.

NOTE ON THE AUTHOR

Ian Martin is an Emmy award-winning comedy writer and producer. His screen credits include the BAFTA-winning BBC series *The Thick of It* (for which he was originally brought in by Armando Iannucci as 'swearing consultant'); BAFTA-nominated *The Death of Stalin* (National Society of Film Critics Award, Best Screenplay); the multi-Emmy award-winning *Veep* (for which he won an Emmy and two Writers Guild of America Awards) and HBO's *Avenue 5*. He also wrote for the Oscar-nominated film *In The Loop*. His comedy-drama *The Hartlepool Spy* won the Tinniswood Award for Best Radio Drama in 2020. He has written for the *Architects' Journal, New Statesman,* the *Observer* and the *Guardian*. His experimental prose poem *PANIC* was set as a GCSE English question in 1998. From 2000–2005 he edited the cult satirical website martian.fm. His previous books include *Epic Space, The Coalition Chronicles* and *Lost In The Attic*. He lives in Lancaster, where he runs a primary school writing workshop. The workshop's first screenplay – *Tig* – was shot and released as a short film in 2024.

NOTE ON THE TYPE

The text of this book is set in Fournier. Fournier is derived from the *romain du roi*, which was created towards the end of the seventeenth century from designs made by a committee of the Académie of Sciences for the exclusive use of the Imprimerie Royale. The original Fournier types were cut by the famous Paris founder Pierre Simon Fournier in about 1742. These types were some of the most influential designs of the eight and are counted among the earliest examples of the 'transitional' style of typeface. This Monotype version dates from 1924. Fournier is a light, clear face whose distinctive features are capital letters that are quite tall and bold in relation to the lowercase letters, and *decorative italics, which show the influence of the calligraphy of Fournier's time.*